What I wrote About You

by
John
Emery

Dedicated

To

You

Contents

" Introduction"

"Music and heaven are in bloom."

Words I wrote that actively described the wonderful associated memory that quickly became a foreshadowing of a band, besides my own Red Stone of Faith, that would change my life and the lives of others. Though, you gotta hand it to Red Stone of Faith: without it, WINTER DAY probably wouldn't exist. Sorry, I just had to throw that in there.

Rewind to November 15, 2008, the day I met the Emery brothers. I was in NYC playing guitar, and Pat came up to me to jam. I looked in his eyes and knew right away that this guy knew what he was doing.

Being a hard rock/grunge-based guitarist, I was blown away by his skills, the same way I'm blown away to this day. His style sounded borderline classical, with tiny hints of acoustic punk – a mix I would have never thought could be concocted, but easy for my ears to swallow.

When that Saturday was over, and I said my good-byes to everyone I met, Patrick introduced me to the one and only John Emery. You might know him as the guy who rode a mountain lion to the top of Mount Everest…or the vocalist of this band and author of this book. Anyway, Pat put in a good word for me, which led John to ask me to write a solo for one of his band's songs. I was more than happy to.

This was back when the band was Black Winter Day, and as the name implies, it was a darker, harsher incarnation. Being a stranger to "acoustic poetry," or whatever you want to call us, I took quite a while to warm up to the style. Like many others, I sat there wondering why John was talking and waiting for him to actually sing something. But the music was my focus. So I wrote an electric guitar solo for a now-forgotten song, "Words Go Unspoken" – the song was the closest out of the other three on the MySpace page (do you feel old now?) to what I was comfortable writing to. When I went to their house to present the solo…well, you know what happens next. This is the Seasons Change story, remember? We walked into that basement and became victims of a 10-minute musical trifecta and wrote one of our more well-known songs.

And everything else that followed after that day has taken the form of our two albums, this book, and thousands of status updates, Tweets, and Reblogs. But what's it really like joining a band where the only other two members have lived with and known each other all their lives?

Considering our different styles, there's either gonna be a strange yet successful fusion of the styles, or one hell of a negative reaction. And we've had plenty of both. I've written quite a few songs that just didn't make the cut for John. They either sounded "too happy" or "arena rock-ish." I was always writing reflective of my feelings...which was, needless to say, upbeat. John sat me down and taught me to put myself into the mind frame of these songs, to willingly mimic the emotion that his lyrics conveyed.

Eventually, I got the hang of it, and we successfully created a "Winter Day" version of me, while most of the rejected instrumentals have found a nice home on Red Stone of Faith's sophomore album. And depending on when you read this, it may or may not be out yet.

John Emery is one of the most talented musicians I've ever worked with. A great vocalist (he doesn't like the title "singer," because that's not what he does) and an even better lyricist. Every line is honest and true, and they come from very personal aspects. He's not creating these stories outta the blue; at some point in his life, he has been either the narrator or the subject of every one of his songs. Except that one where he talks about a trash can baby. He's never been one of those.

Looking back, I'm glad the Words Go Unspoken session didn't turn into a one-time deal. Otherwise I would have missed the chance to both work with some great musicians and make amazing friends. I remember one night talking about this book and he mentioned the first portion of this book was organized from latest date to most recent; I feel it shows and allows us to see the progression of somebody searching for their own meaning. I could talk about John Emery until I'm blue in the face, but no one knows John Emery better than John Emery. So I will say no more and let HIS words speak for himself.

--Joey Taylor

"*Boy Meet World*"

"L.O.S.T"

Kiss me with a medicated smile
I'll hold you with synthetic arms
Because I'm lost
(L)iving
(O)ff
(S)evered
(T)ies
I wandered for years before I realized I had no idea where I was going
You swallowed the end
Before you even started
Does that mean we're doomed from the beginning?
Only if you waste time answering all the wrong questions
The bitter ate the sweet
Before it could touch my tongue
So I forgot what the world looked like
I'd leave all of nothing behind
If I had anywhere to go
But nowhere
For I found the fine line between patience and wasted time
It's tied around my neck
Keeping me off the ground
So thin
I couldn't see it creeping up

"Hairline"

I parted my hair at just the right angle today
So I could see the scar
From days of implanted fears and phobias
I cared once
But you took it out
I wasn't afraid of being myself
But you found a way to remove that
Alongside all the rest
I once knew the definition of finding one's own path
But we took care of that with a road paved in piss
So now my only memory is the smell
Caked over urine in a dusty factory
I put bathmats in a box today
So content, I didn't even notice the blood
Trickling down my forehead
Signaling the end
Cue the laughter
Is it break time? I can't even remember
When I forgot how I got here
What were we talking about again?
Why is my comb stained,
When the sound of 6:45am does nothing but make me sick?

"Mailbox"

Today I refreshed my e-mail inbox
About a hundred times
Expecting somebody to care
What the fuck is wrong with me?
Consider me the Alzheimer patient of common sense
I always forget how little anyone cares
When it's neither them
Nor their problem
The homeless man, not your brother
The drunk, not your father
The addict, not your mother
The whore, not your sister
Look away, son
That's another man's dreams
Also known as his problems
It calms my nerves
Until we get to the end
When I get over the world
That sinks you under
The End...
A made up term for when you leave
But that's not your problem

"A Drive Home"

I used to be infatuated with this one girl
I used to be naïve
Now I'm just lesser so
While still being more of the same in most ways
Still of the same species
Yet she's old and irrelevant
Now I'm ashamed
You're a reminder of who I used to be
A constant fist pounding the face
Of what should have been
I remember every Sunday
I used to drive from my dad's to campus
Focused on the wrong things
Upset by petty flaws
If I only knew the failure I was driving into
It was riding shotgun
A passenger who refused to speak up before it was too late
If only that sun had eaten me whole
Instead of using me to pick out the filth between its teeth
From meals of even lesser people than I

"This Morning"

If you tongue-fuck the end
I wonder what you'd reach around
I woke up to the apocalypse
I woke up to nothing
Why are your eyes portraying such a dismal future?
I burned up the bed prior to reading a chapter in your pupils
Wishing you were fast asleep
Instead of staring into the parts of me
I'd like to cover up with this blanket I'm starting a fire with
So little we knew when so much of it was waiting right under the bed
If it grabbed you under into childhood fears
I'd probably just get up and go
What I should have done so long ago
Have a nice day

"New"

There is not a single doubt in my mind
That we will meet in another life
And we will do this all again
Maybe it's what even keeps me going in this life some days
Yet we will have lost all the lessons we learned here
And we will do it all again
Young and selfish
Tired and hungry
You and I will do this forever
Even then it won't seem so long
Because every time we could learn
Our minds will be wiped clean in a new place and time
The first time will feel like the last
The one I can't quite recall
Have we met before?
Hello
Damn you
Until again
Always
Good day

"A Trail"

How long have you been following me?
I wonder what you know or how you found me
When I never test the length of my own conscience
I just go in one big circle
Head down
Digging my way into the middle of the earth
I wonder if I'll reach far enough to burn
I'll bring you back a piece of hell
It will make you feel at home
Stalk from afar
When I run myself down
I've become a voyeur in my own life
I can't wait to watch this play out
With the script still warm
Sitting in the director's chair
When will I start acting like I have the control I'm afraid of?

"Happiness/Unhappiness"

Sometimes I wonder
What it would be like if I actually captured happiness
Instead of writing about it
Maybe I'd see it at the post office
Or at the pharmacy
See it from a distance and think of approaching it
Lost in thought, happiness approaches me and smiles
The warm kind
The kind that I can hold close on a cold night
Long after we'd departed
We'd talk for a while
Then we'd part
And this is the best answer for me
A conversation
A smile
Before the end
Then I can lie by myself as I am falling asleep
Playing those few moments together over and over
You wouldn't ruin it by being imperfect or selfish
Or making me change my behavior
In those few moments that we'd spend together
I can enjoy all the good parts of you
Happiness
We won't have to show each other our true natures
Our negatives
With this, I can play the parts out myself
The way I want them to go
I'll be in control of the outcome
Even though it shows I don't have a grip on anything
Let alone myself

"Tonight"

Thought about leaving my apartment tonight
I can't seem to conjure up the thick skin I need to, though
Just can't bear it tonight
Or any night, for the most part
Might hear something that catches me
Like a hook in the cheek of a fish
It will keep me reeling and I won't be able to let it go
I'm afraid of how far people can fall
And for one reason or another
I believe that if I hear it, they'll take me down with them
I'll be made aware of the ignorance they spit out at everyone
And I'll be just as guilty as them
The overweight mother screaming
At her poorly behaved daughter in a grocery store
With resentment to the absent-minded father
That ignores the mother of his child
Pondering about his mistress or the Sunday night game
I hate myself for resenting stories I've never heard
But there's a scent in the air tonight
It reeks of loathing
It's been trailing me most of my life
And on nights like this, I can feel it closing in
One day it's going to wrap around my neck and finish the job
Yet with all this tension, I still need the noise I want to hear
Opposed to theirs
I can't go out tonight
Knowing their words may find me an earshot away
They can't wait to sow their seeds in my garden.
Nobody likes keeping misery to him or herself these days
To each their own?
Not in this day and age
We all have our demons
Just manifest them in different ways
Through art and our interests
I find it almost funny that the things we love so much
Are expressing hardships and pain to those we don't love anymore
All these little hurtful variables
I believe that pain has a positive part of our existence

Through our love we give them a part of ourselves
So we may always remember them
Like a poison that needs to be vomited
We turn it into a physical and/or audible manifestation of a mental pain
Release it and give it a reason
It's like pulling a figure out of your dream
Things are less terrifying that way

"Maybe"

People say "You'll never know" like it's a bad thing
Like the worst thing in the world
Is the feeling someone will forever be in the dark about how you feel
I used to think that
Then again, that's the case for a lot of impulse emotions I've had
If you truly wanted them to know
They would
So there's a reason they don't
Maybe you just can't admit it

"It Goes On"

The things I write the most about
What I know the least of
Words can't describe you
There's no definition for the feeling in my throat
When I know you're near me
I think that's why the pen always writes your name
The never-ending quest
To understand you
I've been told inner peace is impossible to find
I wonder if they've ever met you
I believe that's where they got the idea
You're imperfect
That's important
Just like the small moments in time we share
The good ones
That's why I'm writing this
Because it helps me forget all your filth
So I can have a clean image
When I'm scraping the final images I have of you
Just another piece of writing
That's justified and described nothing
The endless inspiration

"Gutted"

Next to my apartment, there's a grocery store
Every single time I walk by it, I see employees on break
Most of them talking into their phones
And rarely to each other
For the first time tonight, I actually listened as I passed by
Back and forth they went
Yelling or laughing about meaningless things
I don't even think they know
Right next to this grocery store
Is a bookstore that went out of business
Every single time I walk by it, I look through the windows
It's been gutted and left empty for the most part
It never changes but I always look
It reminds me of the grocery store employees and their conversations
I doubt they know the impact they made on me
I doubt they notice much of anything while they talk

"Never Ending"

Your face stays with me always
We will never be forever
Nor will our lives
But until my time is done
I will spend it with your face burned into my thought process
You're in much of my art
I use you as inspiration
When you left my life
My path completely changed
I had to start over
Even then I felt you
Burning at all my negative emotions
Even when you were gone
I still used you to get by
To start something over
Today I turn a new page
But I still feel your ink in my pen
Just waiting to vomit my thoughts of you out
I hate myself for it

"What I'll Never Tell You"

I'm sorry you're sick
If you ever read this, you'll feel it's about you
Not because you could know
Rather because you're selfish
Just as selfish as I am
Overdramatic and self-destructive
This is why the words I write in privacy
Will be the closest thing to you being consoled by me
I wonder if I could ever love you again
It's always the same conclusion
Only if you were deaf and blind
Could I ever go back to that time?
Because then you wouldn't even know
Anonymity
The ultimate necessity with you
Inches away from your face
And you wouldn't have a clue
It sounds almost as sick as you are
But I would love to love the you that couldn't see, hear, or speak
Because then you wouldn't fail me
Only then

"Boxes"

If you asked his kids what their father did for a living, they'd tell you he counts boxes
If you asked me what he did for a living, I'd tell you he counts down the days
Before he blows his miserable brains out the back of his head
On the canvas of an unsuspected wall
Not even then will you be able to make sense of his mind
With it right in front of you
Coagulating the sides of some whore house
Happy ending?
I don't think so

"Waste Basket"

I've written a lot of garbage about you
Before this moment, I just couldn't stand the idea of throwing out the rot
The stench is the closest thing
To digging my self-deceit into your neck
And calling it home
This page was once filled
Now all that I remember are black smudge marks
Like the tire streaks of a car trying to avoid swerving off the road
Yet now I'm reporting from a ditch on the side of the road
There's an outline of you from when you flew out the front seat
It is beautiful
The silence lets me know where you are
The broken glass calms my nerves
I may wonder if it hurt and many more things
Yet I can tell you for certain
An outline in broken glass makes me more comfortable than you did
The air comes through where you went
I can hear it howling out my name
Welcoming me back to a page
Daring me to come out on the other side without you
To take out the trash

"Movies Are Bullshit"

My first reaction was to comfort you
It always was
This is something you will never know
I'll stand just beyond the shadows
The point where the sun can't kiss my existence with your view
Always out of sight
I'll watch everybody else do it for you
The urges I'll hold back that have been complacent for so long
You will never know, and it will always be that way
Even now I have known
I have seen the future
And these thoughts never leave my head
Even in my wildest moments
They never have a chance in counter with my tongue
Nor does what comes out have a wild affair with your ears
It just is
Do sleeping dogs lie?
Or do they just bleed out all over their forgotten times?
They don't even realize it
When they're too busy wondering
Back to if there were any sign
It would end like this
When they're thinking back to the start
As they trace over the entry point
Oh, what a wound

"Time"

I can't help but feel that these times are the end of it all
Men leave their homes and sacrifice the self for the whole
Only to return to nothing
After the fact
That they've been beaten six feet deep
So instead
They now rest their heads on motel sheets
And wonder who last fucked here
Whose seed they lay rest on
By the hour
Even when it feels like seconds
When they think, "Why couldn't it be me?"
Maybe because you don't even know what that means
You're a ghost in broken skin
You cast no shadow
Make no difference
Yes, it's the end of time
When you never started the clock
They'll tell you, "We are dying everyday"
But how can that be true when you never started living?

"Pretend"

If I close my eyes tight enough
I swear I could push myself out of this world
Into a new life
With all the knowledge I learned in the old
In this place
I act the way I should
And I somehow control everything we feel
Vanity has been eradicated from your heart
And all my shortcomings shot between the eyes
But once upon a time is set in nowhere
When you're the fairy tale princess of nothing
Because you're still on that corner
You sink in that bed
The worn down world we really live in
Tastes like shame
Feels like even less
Meanwhile I play make-believe
And if anybody passed me by
While I was playing this game
They'd take me for a blind beggar
Grabbing at air
For something that wasn't there
For something that's never coming back

"Towns"

Everybody says, "I hate this town"
It's all just a cover
If it wasn't here, it would be the same thing elsewhere
No matter where you are
You're there with yourself
Until you can wear your flaws on your chest
You're always going to hate where you are
It's always raining within
Watching it from the windows of your eyes
Stop placing the blame
When you just want the attention that follows
Sounding desperate to get out
But you'd have to rip yourself from your skin to do that
And it fits that well for a reason
Wear it well and wear it down
You can't get out of your soul
So stop blaming these streets
They have their own flaws
Their own nightmares to wake up from
You just have to run through the cracks in the ground
Like the ones you make up
To realize that
It's so much simpler than you'd like to admit

"In My Head"

The world is over, and I'm the last one left
Digging graves for all the ones I loved
Staying behind to do them right
Look at me
Lone wolf.
Survivor.
Hero.
It's a strange place
Where even this can be glorified
In our heads
We're never the first ones to die
Always the last one left
Firing off into a crowd of undead
Screaming for victory
Wearing our hurt in our heads
When we're stuck in their worlds
Even pain is glamorized these days
What a world

"Waiting For Trains"

I remember there was a time
When I wanted to write this book
Telling stories inspired by my life
When I'd ride trains into beautiful cities
Meet heroes turned homeless
Strumming out-of-tune guitars somehow still sounding beautiful
Women of such damage, that only their beauty could rival
Conversation of depth
And tales of friendship
I'd ride alone
But never by myself
When in reality
I only ride to the same dead towns
To see the same life suckers every week
We shake hands
They nod
I smile
We talk
It's always small
The smell always rotten
And I can see the garbage between their teeth
The only beauty is when it all comes crashing down
I'd write
Without anybody having to know the truth
Well, except for you and I
Just you and I
Between these pages we'll keep this secret
With the scent of disgust far off in the distance
Yet just strong enough to hint at
When you'd run over these words
Like life ran over the characters I'd describe
So just live in fear
That somebody is going to see right through this bullshit
Even then there would be no truth
Just see through me
See through
It's what I've become
What I have to stop

"Cure"

If you dove into your deep end
You'd break your neck
Everybody seems so much shallower than they'd like to admit
But if we all had to jump into ourselves
We'd understand
When someone shoves us face first into our own piss
When we'd have to smell and acknowledge everything
Then we'd know
That's how you find out who could rise from their ruinous self
And fight anew
Before the wounds can heal
When infection can still crawl in
Let the disease sink into me
We all stumble upon a cure at one point in our lives
It's just a matter of who is willing to take it
And the casualty rate is climbing
Because we're all just sinking
That's why I haven't seen you in so many suns
When I injected myself with all of my wrongs
And let it sit in my blood
That's how I knew
I was becoming immune
To all that you do
When I finally accepted me
Better? Worse?
I don't know

"In My Room (Pt. 1)"

My nerves ache
It means the rain must be coming
Each drop, a word in a water-stained book
It's the downpour
The book I've been writing
The ink bleeds off
Into this drain
I wished I could grab my hand down
And squeeze them back into my head
Instead I just lay with an empty collection of nothing
I read it every night
Fall asleep with the great big nothing lying across my chest
It's bound in nothing
No leather to trace over my fingers when I read my nothings
I used to think I could ride out the storm
Until recently
When I started to taste my broken pen
In the water that tried drowning me
It tasted like a person
A place
A smile
A laugh and a smell
Yet I couldn't place my finger on it
Because I woke up and found I was alone
Sitting and tracing my finger over an empty page in a blank book
As if I was looking for an old friend
Or a memory that changed me

"All. Nothing. Nowhere. (Pt. 2)"

If I were to see your face on a billboard one day
I wouldn't be surprised
Nor if I walked by to see those two dead eyes staring at me from the gutter
You're an all-or-nothing person, or so you make me feel
I give it all
Now I feel like I'm nothing
But that is selfish and self-defeating
I am thicker than the skin you've peeled away
Thicker than the shame I need to push away
So if we meet in the stars or down by the gutter
I'll walk on by
With the thought, taste, and foreign memory
Of a person I once knew
In a place
At a time
With only one thing in common
They no longer exist
And in the distance
I hear the storm drain water
Just low enough to hear
Far off enough to breathe in the smell
My footsteps try to drown it out
As I try and recall what and who I was just thinking about

"Delivery"

People put such meaning in quotes
They try to capture a moment and a feeling
So they may reflect it on others
The genuine connection
The unknown bond between author and reader
Person to person
Yet how many times have the thoughts of one
Been mangled by the many?
It doesn't matter, the beauty of the meaning
When I'm cursing the messenger
You can hide behind the beauty in them
But the ugliness always shines through
You can write me these letters
I can read the words
But the disgust I feel when I run over the envelope
That I knew was licked shut by such a foul tongue
Will always stay with me the longest
It will fill my entire head
I won't wash it off
When I never throw it out
I give such meaning to objects that can't move
So I don't have to feel what it is I should be dealing with
I'll just think of how you once held what I now obtain
And how I love the ugliness
As much as it disgusts me
It's easy
I need to start learning the hard way

"Photos"

Cop-outs and faux friends
Where do I begin?
How I've let people make me feel, when will it end?
There's no reason and the words don't rhyme
I've lost myself in the thoughts of others
And tried to make a career out of it
You burn out when you should shine through
And I lost myself in the dark, trying to help you find the sun
My eyes tells the tale better than I can
But I won't let you look at me
So file this under "mystery" and let's leave it at that
Lets never meet again
None of us need to make this any more sour than it's already become
Drink this on the rocks and let it burn down
I hope the hole in your heart matches the one you all make in the stomach
How funny I find it when I look at pictures
I think of what could have been
And what never was to pass
Rather than the times we all had

"A Moment to Myself"

Your tears slipped right through my hands
I had the entire car ride home to think about the dropped pass
I hate those moments
Where you can't help but focus on the "could have been"
The one that makes you feel like everything is ending
The world's not as tragic as our personal hurt feels
I stop
I go
And still this feels endless
Even when I know the end is in sight
"I'll never forgive you"
"Yeah, we'll see soon enough"
I wish I didn't know me
So I could act surprised when I fall into the same bad habits
When I can't catch you
When you fall through the cracks
The ones too thin to dive into
Or so I think
When it's too late to call anyone
When the roads lay deserted
The time when even the radio is too much for your ears to handle
Just the road and the thoughts you can't turn down
The ones that seem to lay in comfort
When you know that old habits die too hard
Too soon
When you're not ready to stop
Either you leave the abuse
Or become too numb to it
The hardest lesson for me
Was finding the difference
Between a thick skull and a beaten one
They're never the same. Not ever.

"A Home to Hang From"

With the book of slander in my hand
And the noose around my neck
Don't kick the chair before I can
Speak the good word that sounds wrong
When it was nursed from spite
It will never heal
As it's kicked from under me
Now we swing

"Vain"

I saw myself and tried pulling out familiar words
Looking for similar replies
But the silence filled every square inch between the mirror and I
The air hit hollow holes
It infested the inside
The only thing I ever found in you
Is now the first thing I discover in the morning
I watched you sink the clouds as you rose above
And I would have joined you
But the weight of realism keeps me tied down to another day
I bet I'm better off
But it's always easier said than done
Especially now that I understand
Good luck on your journey

"Illness"

I wonder if the planet will ever figure out a way to get rid of us
Throughout our history of being a disease that finally found a home
It's tried
Plagues and disease
Our cries are the success of this world
The quicker they do away with us
The better the chance this planet has of survival
Maybe your god is a scientist
Who created cancer to save the planet
Your death is another step towards the salvation
Of the earth you waste upon
Save your spiritual beliefs for somebody else
I'm just a walking disease

"Concrete Grave"

I can't tell if the broken pavement is telling me that it's had enough
Or if it's just waiting to find a new start
All I know is that it breaks off more and more
Until I wonder if it will break open and I'll fall into the earth
I'll rest my head in the dirt and I'll be surrounded by the dark
Close my eyes and lose all insecurity
Under a blanket completely surrounding me
I try so hard to glorify all this bullshit
When I'm thinking this crazy concept
I'm just another twenty something kid
On a New Jersey street
Nobody sees anything out of the ordinary
They never look down at the ground
They forget the cracks
They don't see what I see
They'll never fall right through
When you can't find the warmth
You'll have sworn the cold is all you know
And you're breaking off all you ever could have been
Or at the least, it's what I'd like to think
Until I feel the cool air rub my shoulder
Caress my neck
As it digs into my spine and makes me shudder
We all like to think we can avoid the fate of everybody else

"In and Out"

It amazes me
How many people we pass everyday
The stories behind them, a mystery
We treat them like they're diseased
As they do us
No eye contact
We might as well be blind
Might as well see empty sockets with maggots weaving in and out
I may have just passed the greatest love I could have known
My best friend, my worst enemy
But now we're nothing and we will never be more
What a shame
The irony is too bitter
All these people
Forever closed off
Containing the greatest pains I would have listened to
Now it's just the enlightenment I lost
When we all just keep to ourselves
When there's so much we should be speaking
Blind and deaf
Emotionally crippled
This can't be healthy

"The T.V."

I saw a young woman on the TV today
Sixteen at most
The princess was crowned with two black eyes that almost consumed her face
She spoke between long pauses
That bridged together a story
Of an abusive boyfriend
An absent father
An addict mother
She tells of only shunning and exposing her abuser
When a female celebrity announced that she had been beaten
Only then did she feel like she should leave the abuser behind
"Oh, what an inspiration she was!"
I'm sick and physically upset by this
Is this the world we live in?
Where the rich and celebrated can only inspire
The things that common sense should have screamed
I'm sorry for your pain, young lady
Nobody deserves such hurt
But money is a construction that we have the blueprint to
It's all manmade
And it biologically enhances nothing
Your life is just as priceless as the rich
Same as the poor
I'm sick of false idols
Spewing from the gospel of the green
Life is an equal value type of game
Yet nobody seems to know the rules

"Colorblind"

If black is truly the absence of all color
Your heart hasn't seen a lick of light in my lifetime
Then again, scientists and children all have different answers
For which is the absence of color and light
So I'm just left with whatever metaphor adds up for your frustration
It hurts to see
But more so to hear
A lifeless croak
From a dying dog
If only you knew what I burned without you
The red and the yellow entwine around the small of your back
And they kiss the ear with the burning it can hear
I'd take you with me if I thought it would make a difference
But that ship sailed into the blue a long time ago

"First Work Day of the Year"

It is 6am
First Monday of the year
And the only thing I can think is,
"One day, if even one person read this, I know it would be enough"
Still, I am instead driving down the same roads
Every weekday at dawn
It's not paving away to the future I was told
Just streaked with ice and blackened snow
I can't afford much gas these days, so I am taking it slow
I can't stand how mad I get at all those who pass me
Using your blinker seems to be a foreign idea these days
And it racks nerves normally reserved for issues of a more prominent nature
New Years resolutions seem impossible
When I'm focused on the everyday resolution
To not be so petty, bitter and insecure
So I think
As I find myself surrounded every morning
By those who tell their families it's a job they hate
An environment that leaves them helpless
I hope the forty-five seconds they save getting there helps them find salvation
This is all I think of as I am punching in
Maybe that is why after two years
My time card looks so scattered
So I'm going to sit down
Look busy
Glue my eyes to the clock
Write e-mails
And wish I was writing books
That could be protected and bound in hardcover
Telling tales of the best of friends and the worst of times
Just so I could connect with someone
Simply because nobody ever reads the e-mails of a customer service rep
Trust me
I sent out one hundred plus, and I'm staring at an empty inbox
I have found a home in people's spam folders
Old friends and I are losing each other
And leaving behind dust-coated paper trails
Bands break up

Pages stay empty
At the very least, though
Our girlfriends can tell their parents about our stable jobs
We'll impress them
They'll smile
This is where we stop living for ourselves
A slope so steep
I hope I can climb up
That I can dig my fingernails
And climb back up into my own thoughts
Every day it gets harder, and this should be obvious
Driving down these same roads home
Deeper and deeper into routine
Going home to try and recharge
Dreading tomorrow
As I'm cut off by another middle-aged man
He's racing home to his wife
Isn't this the same man that always complains to his co-workers about that
same woman?
The one they make fun of after they're done eye fucking the college girls
working at D&D?
If that water cooler could talk, eh?
Go home
Make a drink
The 6pm *Sportscenter* depends on you
All I am is some kid
On some street
Working some job
Trying to grow into a better man

"Man Meets Failure"

"Fiend"

Culture fiend
You'd eat death if I painted it pretty enough
Spoon-fed feast that you don't understand
And your hunger doesn't have an end
Excess doesn't exist in the land you lay
Ladies and gentlemen
We're at the end of an era
So now I step aside
I will watch you all from afar
Sit back and wonder this:
So much is going right at this moment
Without any of you to see it
Making you wrong for all the best reasons
I've lived as a fool among thieves for so many years
We laughed together with one cheek
While you beat me on the other
Had one arm around me to console
With the other diggin' for gold
Culture fiend needs a new fix
I ain't no dream dealer
But that didn't stop you from taking me for a ride
It may have been beautiful
But it left me breathless for so long, I started to suffocate
Smiling with a purple face
You pressed the gun to my head and said it wasn't loaded
You pressed the gun to my head and said…
But even if it was
Wouldn't that be fun?
Culture fiend
Left the crime scene
But I know 'em well enough to guess he's itching for the next
I'll see you in my dreams, culture fiend
I won't wish you well
I'll just wish I never woke up from this illusion
Cause it was so much easier than what I am left with

"Weak End"

Last night I dreamed about where I was going when I'd wake up
What a waste of a good night's sleep
Drained and delusional
I drove my car to the end, with my past riding shotgun
It turned the radio up too loud
The heat too high
Yet it never drowns out the noise between us
Or quiets these chills
There's so little to think about this early, and it's never good
Because it's always the truth
It's so loud in here
The whisper still rings in my ears, though
Like snakes weaving in between each other
The words take hold of my senses
Anxiety is only motivation for synthetic needs
Lies for the liar
A demented idea of what somebody told me today
Between their smile
I could have sworn I saw a snake made out of money crawl down their throat
Too quick to see
Before I could grab it up out of you
How did it taste going down?
I hate to keep using the word "bitter," but I bet that's how it felt
If it weighs too heavy on your stomach
Can you vomit up change for a dollar?
Choosing the dollar over the change you need
It's a snake-eat-snake world
When we're all so green
What was that about anxiety again?
It seems so lost when I'm up so early
For something so ageless
Meaningless
Endless

"Homeless Illusion"

She drank your insecurity
And spit it back up as fire
She loved to drink and she loved to dance
I used to think she'd dance on everyone's grave
Many years passed
And her presence was now just a far forgotten memory
Until I saw her
Homeless and smelling of piss
I could have sworn her hair was made of snakes
They bobbed and weaved lustfully in between each other
And on top of her head
She was laughing
On her knees
Begging
For a dollar
A bullet
A minute of your time
Or anything in between
I tried to speak but couldn't find any words to do the goddess mess justice
She became sick and vomited on the sidewalk
She dug her fingers into her own regurgitated filth and began writing patterns
They told the future
I saw me
I saw her
And everybody else in the world
Under a blazing sky
Waiting to sink us down
Our blood running through the cracks in the sidewalk
Hiding from the firefight
With vomit still crawling out of her mouth like a maggot
Seeing the sun from under a rock for the first time in days
It dripped unto her utopia
Her portrait of madness
It reeked of self-loathing
She continues to laugh and pulled the snakes from her head
I was convinced
Nobody else was
All they saw was a homeless whore picking clumps of her hair from the roots

Vomiting from drug sickness
I saw the end
I felt the sadness
My eyes met the guilt of a girl
Who loved to dance but for too long, pissed on her own grave

"I Feel Trapped"

I hate knowing what is going on in a world
That I must share with you
I try and starve myself of all the useless words
But there's just not enough substance to keep me well-fed
When I'm breaking past the point
Where anything you say even makes sense
And the ringing in my ears
Is telling me I can't love you anymore
That I can't love you in this world
That I can't love this world
The one I pretend we don't share
Miles apart
Never felt so close
When I can't escape my own thoughts
You don't have to be near
The faintest of pulses
Need not even find itself in a host
For you are rotting me out
Nothing I say even makes sense
Losing brain cells
Losing sight
Losing time
Lost myself
And
If beauty is in the eye of the beholder
I'll push my thumbs so far into your skull
When I'm losing possessions
Out the window
Losing perception
From the center of where this fire started
The eyes that could put it out
Blind
And if I thought before I spoke
I'd be as quiet as you were blind
The beauty we no longer see
The days we no longer speak of
The painting that dried
Hear no evil, see no evil

Cementing my opinion of you
This singular moment of time
Where we spoke in watercolor paint sets for kids
But I drowned in the smell
Of genocide
Of the self
The whole
The almighty
One
You
Seemingly perfect
The art of fooling everybody perfected

"You Bleeding Heart"

Be still, my beating fucking heart
Before I beat it out of you
Out of me
I never truly let it out
When the words never leave me
Even though the heart quickens when answers are so far away
I always end a line
The final one
Right before we're about to get to the heart of a solution
There just isn't enough of me to care
If there ever was, I'd leave
Before your bleeding heart could leak a trail to follow
Breadcrumb paths for the love-struck
Get eaten up by predators who sense the salt in the blood
Dripped by somebody who got too close
I can't be that victim
Because I could never give myself up
Let my hiding spot be seen
For the chance to get caught
To feel hurt
The possibility of having your nails rip away my face
I don't want you to think what I think
See what I see
Feel how I feel
Bleeding and beaten or broken and still
Who knows?

"Tools for Lying"

I ripped your tongue out
So I could try and find where the lies began
To see if there's a treasure map that leads to the jackpot
The reason for you
I didn't find a thing
So I'll leave you to pick up the pieces
Of what little life remains
As I wrote the above mentioned
I imagined it playing out on the baseball field
Behind my childhood friend's house
I don't know why
In fact, we could go as far as saying that I don't know a thing
However, I wrote this and honestly imagined ripping out
The thing that lied the most
And throwing it down on a dust-plagued baseball diamond
Walking away while a four-finger-wide stream of blood ran down your chin
Politically speechless
In this fantasy you have finally forgotten
All that was needed was to take away everything about you
That made you yourself play ball

"Dirt Words"

Have you ever thought to yourself,
"I wonder if all gods go to Heaven?"
Well, how about we let the dog bury his bone
Underneath (all) the good book(s) and see what burns first
An old man once told me,
"I bet it's a lonely light when we come to the end."
I didn't have the heart to tell him
That I wasn't so sure it was any worse than what the world faced on a daily basis
He made me think of Dante and his work in the Comedy
Rumor had it, men of his time feared him
Because his writings spoke with the confidence that he had seen Hell
I believe he did, but it was only inside of himself
The masses fear someone who can look inward
And say the faults were of his own doing
I wonder if I would have stayed away with the rest
In truth
I think I would just be jealous
Yet being a human being means I'm absorbed in the self
And foolish enough to ask,
"Who has the better songs: God or the Devil?
On my way up or down, it would be nice to enjoy the elevator music
I hear the Devil has all the greats
While God is jamming techno/dance tracks
And the plug to the record player can't stop fucking the outlet
And I'm left with an empty hall
So who burns first: the bone or the word?
The needs of the man or the words he came up with?
You're telling me it's some divine speech
Yet if it's all man-made
How can we know what's above and beyond?
Or so below
You can't know a single damn thing
That isn't in front of your dog damned given face
I'm not saying you're right or wrong
Just a simple request that you practice not preaching
What not one of us on this earth could even begin to know

"I Wish We Tried Harder"

I got a name for every letter in the alphabet of a person I lost
And I wish that hit list was shorter
'Cause today it took me two hours just to start writing from a pure place
And the lack of purity I found looking outward was so short
You wouldn't see it if you were looking straight
Which leaves me singing off-key, half written from my heart
And the other half coming somewhere from
When you updated a social networking site that won't matter in five years
Because you felt compelled to feel the same way as the friend laughing next to you
I want an original thought to shake up the way you think
'Cause the last time I saw you walking my way
Down on into my life
It was someone I barely recognized
And I don't know what I'm trying to say
But right now my fingers fly faster than the sky
Or faster than my mind can hope to think
And I hope it comes out in a half-coherent manner
But today it took me so long to write
When it's so easy to find thoughts pre-written by the rest of the world
The way people think reminded me of when I was a little boy
And I would get sick with the flu every winter
Like clock work
When the days got shorter
While the cold made them feel so much longer
The pit of my stomach would ache
And for hours I'd toss and turn on my childhood bed
Wrestling for space and comfort with my stuffed bear
The one with both arms sown from surgical operations performed by my mother
Cause my love for the guy had ripped off his arms too many times to count
I learned to love things to death from an early age
But anyway…
After hours I finally threw up the Gushers my dad told me I shouldn't have eaten
The soup, my mother promised, would make me better
And I think the day-old expired orange juice my little brother dared me to drink
I did it because I used to think being the bigger brother meant facing more terror
Even if that was just slightly-off-tasting juice
So that's what it was like writing today
Like throwing up as a child

As it was when I was afraid of the dark
The phobia of seeing a stuffed bear's arm come off
Because when you're six, you could swear the things you feel most sincere about
Can feel all the pain you would
Had you been in their shoes
That moment just now
That I connected with today
Was way before I had the alphabet hit list of broken hearts
Before I could give you every single letter known to man
With a name of somebody that I missed
Of an emotion that didn't feel quite right
It took me a minute to realize that when everything I read by my peers was wrong
I wish we felt for ourselves
I know we have it in us
To go back to the moments in time
Where the soft fuzz coming out of a limbless stuffed toy
Could bring us to our knees before we knew pain
We knew a lot more than we thought
Way before you replaced it all with worry
Over what somebody may or may not have written about you
On a day where you did nothing for yourself but wither away

"Hands"

If the only thing we truly know is what we create
I'm left with a lot of lost words that tried finding comfort on a computer
That most often finds rest in a corner cubicle
At a job I don't care to write anymore about
If all we really know is what we create
I'm writing for my own salvation
In a kingdom I haven't finished creating
Based off of disgust for all the beautiful things in this world
That self-destructs itself
For the greater good of nothing
For reasons unknown to me
When I don't build to add to that world
It's a lonely feeling
When your emotions jump up to the gateway of your throat
The moment when the idea of losing everything you didn't create
Is shoved right in your face
It's the time when I'm forced to see how fragile you really are
How close it is to ending
I should have known better
But I got too comfortable in a world I wasn't built for
There isn't any dirt on my hands here
So I guess I should get to leaving

"Fou-Roux, Where is Your Ear?"

If you ever wondered why Van Gogh cut off his ear
You've probably never spent a second
Let alone years
Having your profession be the art
Of trying to get the world to view itself as you do
Maybe the thought was just too small
I'd decapitate my head if I decided to severe all ties
So let's start at the base and then see if you'd take the time to understand
When you really find yourself, you lose everything else you're apart of
That's the point I feel, and now I'm better off for it
I'd rather scream alone
Than whisper in your crowd
You can try to put a bullet in your brain
You might just make it out alive
When you're made of iron, it can be hard to crack
But the smallest tear in your belief
Will rip you apart
The faith that was never there
Always translates to the most forgettable words
That can describe the majority of the people you'll meet
It's never good to be misunderstood, until they accept that as well
They'll throw stones until the cuts and bruises are fashionable to them
Then, I recommend escaping while they start bashing their own brains in
You could dare them to beat some sense into their skulls
But they'd miss the point
So this is what you get yourself into every time you write
Maybe I'm better off unknown
Under the radar doesn't seem like such an isolated home anymore
Not when I realize the sharks I'd be swimming with
And all the fish guts I'm dressed in
Lend me your ear before I give you mine
It makes sense
If nobody gave you a penny for your thought
Or passion
Everything you truly loved
When they do
It's never longer than a glance
Or just enough air to rip it apart

"All Mine Alone"

All my favorite songs have the word love in them
All my favorite holes are dripping blood
Off the center of foreheads
All my favorite friends are finding homes in the laughter of others
While I make my bed in irrelevancy
As good a home as any when you have nowhere else to go
Everything you love looked as if it may have been familiar one day
That isn't close to a date I'd mark off on my calendar
I feel like apologizing, but I don't know what for
Should I send the letter to a mailbox I can't remember?
The asking of questions to try and get around the answers only I could have
A shame we've come to this point
I'm ashamed to no longer be a part of this
The immune system did its job
And I'm a disease looking to sink into the sun of another
Taking all applicants
Come with a lot of baggage
With an even bigger mouth
And dirty laundry stained with disappointment
Cold or warm water won't rinse this away
When you're stuck with the shame
Please respond today

"Showering in the Dark"

If you were deaf and blind
Then we could truly find the answer to the questions of life
Because you wouldn't be filled with the garbage you stuff your senses with
Not when everything has been severed
When all you have is darkness and the ideas from your head
You are perfect, the truest form of beauty
An island unto yourself
The entity known as you
Nothing foreign enters through the face
No intruders break into your mind and fill you
With nonsensical insecurities that gnaw on your brain for days
There are moments when I close my eyes and shower in the dark
With nothing but me
Calming and free
I look in the mirror and I hate that I have taken in much of what I loathe
I can repeat television jingles and identify campaign mascots
Quicker than people I have actually met before
So much trash passes through this mind
More decayed than useful
I'm just trying to salvage these thoughts
My sanity and maybe a small amount of credibility
I told my mother the other day
Driving down Route 78
We can never know us
Or the meaning of life
Nor God, the Devil, or the world in between
Not when since as long as we can remember
Since our senses and memory came together to form our opinions
Have been infiltrated by others
It reminded me to take a look inward
To see what was real and what had been placed there
But I never did
I couldn't face what culture and society had done to me
It made more of me than I want to confess
I wonder if these words are mine
I can't tell you
Nor do I think I could
Deaf and blind vs. numb and medicated

"Backpacks"

Today was an interesting day
My brother came over to my apartment
Laid himself on the couch like a therapist's patient
It's too bad I didn't have any credentials to listen
Or give advice that isn't mentally self destructive
With his shoes on the furniture
(An offense I've given him at least three warnings about)
He starts telling me this story
About how he was eating lunch at his college today
I imagined him in a corner alone
Eating fried food with his iPod across the table
Like the better half he hasn't known
Looking as antisocial as possible
Or so I assume
He sees all these young kids on a field trip to the school
Kids of maybe six, seven, or eight
Children who don't know a world of Super Nintendo
Or the original cast of 'All That"
Wide-eyed, bright, and beautiful
Without the heavy burden of giving up
On a new day that they're aware is so close
Over-hearing them talk, he tells me that what they're most excited about
Is getting to see "all the big kids" with backpacks that look too heavy to carry
And books the size of their baby brothers and sisters at home
Everything is new
Nothing has the effect of "been there, done that"
They don't see that kid as a burnout who could care less if he ever found
A hint of knowledge or an ounce of education again
The girl who sleeps around and is followed
By pessimistic whispers and words spat
No…
Things like that
Are so much less real than the monsters under their bed
Or all the figures that only appear when the lights go out
The same figures that are only afraid of flashlights and dads
All they can see is the most beautifully simplistic ideas that surround them
Things that, as you grow older, are seen as trivial and worthless side notes
To other (and clearly) more worthwhile news bits about who is sleeping with who

Or the kid who overdosed in high school
With a laugh and an open bottle of beer
We swallowed the childhood thought process
Without a wince or a second glance back
So as my brother is telling me this
With his goddamn shoes on my couch
He looks me dead in the eyes and tells me,
"It's such a damn shame that they're going to grow up
To probably become a part of the machine they aren't even aware of."
The fear of big, black and beige backpacks that are sans pictures of superheroes
Filled with books that have print the size of ants in a farm
On an innocent boy's desk at home
Those thoughts will be wiped clean and this slate will be replaced by filth
Now, back to my brother...
I don't know if it was the words he used that struck a distorted chord with me
That rang out with what felt like fifteen minutes of ear shattering feedback
Or if it was the way he said it
The moment we lost eye contact and he fully realized
The level of the thoughts he had just shared
The moment of silence we had
Which carried so much more weight
Than any hollowed sound we could have said at the moment
But I did think
That the world is a beautiful place
But I've watched the casualty count rise
Behind eyes that just woke up one morning
And
Gave
The
Fuck
Up
I wasn't there that day at school
I don't know the names of any of the kids my brother saw
The only faces I can put to them are the ones I make up myself
But that day stuck with me
And since we're being so honest with each other right now
I lied
This didn't happen today but rather weeks ago
I just wasn't sure if I had the ability to write about it

Or do it justice
By a death penalty known as the Delete key
Always dangerously close to my right index finger
Like an executioner who can't wait to watch heads fly
I don't know where we go wrong
You, me, or anybody else you know
From wide eyes to spread legs
There has to be a better way to go about this life
I don't have the answer
I just have the feeling in my heart that sinks
Like a ship in the most sincere of storms
When I hear about kids who have nothing more
Than a clean conscious and an outlook that is as bright as they are afraid
Of a backpack that is too big to carry all the promise
Of a beautiful tomorrow

"The Colder Months of 2009"

1.

Laid on top of me, looking for hope
Even though every path I lead you down showed you something broken
This taught me that mixing the lost with the broken
Is only going to get you a bleak picture that dries
Before it can say anything of value
I remember feeling disgusted that I couldn't feel as disgusted as I should
It was over, but it wasn't done
She wore my t-shirt and it was inches from kissing the skin on her knees
I was inches from kissing the face of obscurity
The destination I should have seen coming
But being young and self-absorbed has a way of clouding judgment
She leaned up against a pool table and I knew what that smile meant
It was a prelude to the pit of my stomach dropping to broken feet
Without a rope leading up to safety
Even though that word meant nothing in this house
The broken-into home
I had told her to park the car in the garage
I lied about the reason
Responding with a smile and not a question or care in the world
Should have been my first sign
Reading through the word "BEWARE" I walked on
We went back upstairs
There was a record playing
Next thing I know it was an hour later
Didn't hear a thing
Or feel any touch
All I could have wished for was dead skin all over
To keep that numbness going
We met in a park weeks later
She was happy and spoke at great length
All I saw was her long jet-black hair
And how I wanted to strangle myself with it
That's all I remember from that day
Passing a gas station and almost hearing her talk
Thinking, "What a wonderful end
To wrap her scent around my throat."

2.

There was so much lost in those months
It took me two and a half years to admit that
To say it was my own fault
So many of you carried me for too long
You should have jumped ship long ago
But I was too busy calling for the heads of traitors
When I should have seen myself for the Judas I'd become
I was no prince or unfortunate royalty
Wrongdoings and rash decisions
The only people I had left
The last thing that was on my mind
Would you call it delusional or selfish?
Who was the winner?
It doesn't matter when nobody is around to see the results
Months later as Spring began
I remember calling my best friend
I half-heartedly apologized for my behavior
He half-accepted it
And the friendship has never been whole since
The silence in between told enough of the story
With me left to wonder what was worth it
Years later, I can finally answer the question
Only now that I see that I'm still dealing with my actions
Some doors just won't close because you broke the hinges
Don't be surprised when the cold comes in
The wind knocks your life over and leaves you empty
Nobody asked for me to do this
Nor did they care when I finally got it
Not that they owed it to me
I wanted to do my past injustice, justice between these lines
Falling short to every standard I'd set
I leave it here
Good, bad, horrible
I'm too jaded and self involved in it to tell
But it had to be said and I'll leave it here
I'll be lucky if I bring myself to edit or read it again
Leave the mistakes in
You all know I'd done that for so long anyway

"Remakes Ruin Things"

All I remember from that weekend was the drive there
And walking those Boston streets while you slept
On certain days, I can't stand this time of year
There is a hint of names no longer relevant
In every morning that was warmer than the last
The constant reminder that there is a moment in time cemented
A period of months where I was not the best human being I could be
It's not even you that I miss
But the opportunity I had
To be a better man
In which I fell short
I'm not a fisherman throwing you back to sea
The hook of responsibility still lays firm in your cheek
I am right there with you
Two peas in a pod
Two sea serpents reeled in with a fishing rod
Our best moments are filled with agony and insecurity
I remember the drive home from that bar
You dumped me on the side of the road by my car and went right back
I didn't blame you for that
The guilt lied on the prints on my fingertips
Where they gripped the door and walked out
If you'd told me that then, I would have called you a liar
It would have been justified if you said the same
I remember that diner
You wore my shirt
I sported the wounds
Hangover hell fight
Fighting words still trying to punch their way out of my lips
My tongue trying to whip its venomous sound against my teeth
I was so engulfed in my pity
Alienating you by watching you flinch at my words
Made me feel beautifully alone
But it was ugly, and I was so full of it
Bullshit and bull spit
The ground floor of us was molded in truth and potential
But the blueprint for the rest was crumbled and torn
Leaving me alone on a train one May morning

With nothing but the floor plan of what could have been
I spent that day in New York
Not knowing where you were
I remember apologizing a while later
It felt as idle and worthless as every other one I'd sent
To you and others alike
You did the same
It was as flat as mine, and we agreed silently
All I remember from that day
Was how my forehead was resting on the seat
The way the sun hit my cheek as I walked the street
Wondering who was in that hotel room in Boston right now
Who they were
And what they were like

"Life Changes (Part 1)"

We say "happy birthday" like we care
And make facial expressions of sadness at funerals like they mean something
Good to know that love means forever,
If by love you mean insecurity
And by forever, you mean only accidentally running into each other
Or at awkward reunions that came too late
Or at grocery stores where I thank whatever is out there
For playing some 80s radio station so I don't have to hear the nothing between us
I can tune out the truth rearing its often ugly mouth to my ear
While telling me so much with so little
Grip the cart a little tighter
Rush your words out a little faster
All while taking small steps away from each other
Smile politely
Try not to show too much pity
Do anything but be honest
Because those days are gone
Especially when we'll never go running back
When we're too afraid we'll get rejected
In this room swimming with eyes we either used to know
Or are only somewhat familiar with
Drown me in social anxiety
So I can throw up these days' end
Make a photo album of filth
It's simple enough
Beautiful days get tainted when they're no longer close enough
When numbers, sunrises, and sunsets have separated us far apart
From when we felt some sense of ease around each other
All the joys of being a bitter old man without having to live in that life
I should have seen it coming, but some things are better left uncertain
We used to know how we felt
Open
Honest
Before the Father, the Son and the Holy Ghost of what keeps me away
If only we knew what we'd become

"Grass Withers (Part 2)"

I didn't even have to think
The road from yours to mine always knew where to take me
Even though I rest my head on different worries these days
Things were different this time
The bumps uneasy
I could have sworn the road was waiting for the right moment to devour me whole
Make me in the midst of the gravel and dirt that fell through its small cracks
I felt uneasy when I used to be the most calm
A cold night and too much traffic
Yet the double yellow lines looked only at me
Knew I wasn't supposed to be here anymore
Knowing they wanted to throw themselves up off the road and tie themselves around me
And shake every memory I had out of me
Tell me never to return
Times like these let me think of the fractures in facades
The hollow frame of golden memories
Only then do I admit to being part of the guilty party
Maybe it's the only thing I do alongside you anymore
When I look for watermarks on photos I barely remember
Then again, the fingers that run over them barely resemble my own
If my main concern is finding somebody to blame
I suppose I haven't even addressed the real problem yet
You all were the crown jewel in a burning palace
Yet now it's missing on the throne rebuilt
I left these walls and told you,
"I miss you all, for what it's worth."
That silence was all that greeted me
Giving me just enough time to sit alone with that thought
All that came to mind was how sick to my stomach I felt
This time I didn't have a public soundtrack of laughter, radios, and conversation
To drown out the feelings I knew I was burying
Now I've ran out of dirt and space
At this moment, that doesn't seem like the most promising of answers

To the most unsettling of questions
All I'm left with:
Life changes
Grass withers

"Headcase"

Spring used to bring so much more
The garbage this garden has become
Is only a part of the problem
So when the filth is in full bloom
It always smells the same and leaves me here
Human beings are so flawed, it's terrifying
Or they're beautiful beyond words
I don't know which it is
I can't tell if associating our memories with buildings, seasons, places, and things
Makes us better or worse
It weakens my blood to remember
But it's only when I have even less (or nothing left)
Am I of the weak, seeking shelter for something that holds no value?
Or am I the last hope I need to be searching for?
I always hate writing and looking back
To find more question marks than periods
When the beginning doesn't show promise
We always expect people to stay for the encore
It's easy to be your own worst enemy
I try not to think about these things
But the only questions left to ask are
"How terrible are people?"
"How much do they truly disappoint?"
When they don't live up to the expectations we create
I've mismanaged so many people in my life
Mistaking them for who I wanted them to be
When I should have just seen them for who they really were
Leaving me with only myself to blame
Shallow friends and strong drinks won't drown your memories
They're hell-bound and fireproof
Made for war and built on survival
Only time can kill what you've made up in your head
They only leave when you do
You can't outrun yourself
You can't outlive the lies

"Tongue-Tied Luck"

Out of the loop when I'm out of luck
Both sides of the coin burned off the steel
Heading for the tail end of us
When the debt is too much to collect
We grab and run
A fistful of a new life
Hoping that something we held on to will be better than the last
In opposite directions we flee
Leaving little pieces of time that fell from our palms
I grip onto something I've never even known
Heels kicking up enough dirt to cloud my judgment
So I won't have to think these thoughts
When you're still in my eyes' reach
Do you wonder if the back of my foot will spring me farther away?
Or if it's just taking me in a circle
Slowly digging me in place
Things don't look so familiar at this angle
Self-defeating to the point that I'm hoping the dirt will drive so far into my
ears
I won't hear the time you're having
I think I dropped everything I reached for, while I was running in place
I'm glad we talked
More so that it wasn't on a landline
So I didn't have a cord to choke mistake-ridden words with
What's the penalty for destroying your own tongue?
Whispers on the streets and nothing among the sheets
But I'm choking on the words and no way to ask for help
That time has passed
Now that I think about it
Time is a funny thing
So is how I view it
We don't get enough of it
Yet I still kill so much of it
With nothing but a deep dark hole for show
How about a penny for your thoughts?
When there's nothing tongue-in-cheek about you

"Fabricated"

Too many tears claimed as our own
When we don't even know where the eyes begin and the mouth ends
Nothing about that is beautiful
The definition of glory is miscommunicated and lost in translation for the
young
I can't believe what this has come to
The we, as a collected whole
We do each other wrong but scream for the blood of others
When we pick the scabs of our own wounds
How badly do you want the scars?
The definition of a badge of honor is so distorted
I'm surprised you can get a signal in this shithole
Doing ourselves wrong in shadows
Blaring hate speech towards others in the light
As the years pass by like crippling déjà vu
I wonder what it is we'll create
With venomous spit and a dictionary mouth
Ready to spew out bitterness in its many forms of guilt
It's amazing what you can do with a condescending smile and a wag of the
finger
The tree grows from love and attention
We are what grew from self-doubt
Hanging sideways
Ready to fall at any time
With a hollow inside that could break with the wrong turn of the wind
Look at your roots
Find the corroded
Watch the leaves fall

"Doctor"

My hands decided to play surgeon
Everything they dissected kept coming up cancer
The diagnosis told me that fragmented goodbyes of half-hearted eyes
Couldn't wait to escape that which wasn't going to heal
It looks pretty fatal right now
And the half-forgotten are starting to fade completely
It doesn't seem to be the worst thing that could have happened

"Berkeley Heights"

Berkeley Heights, the dying whore
They closed down the pharmacy
The pizzeria
The movie theatre
Gasoline Alley
I had my first birthday there
Blowing out a single candle while the town lost its final spark
I'm convinced we're all just hypocrites exposing ourselves at different angles
and times
You'll shake my hand with a shit-eating grin and hide your town secrets
Blow your brains off and consider it a life well lived
I wonder if you died with that smile on your face
Or if death itself was the only thing ripping the truth off a thick skull
Like a scalp begging to be taken from the head
Either way, there's no more lies
Not when fundraisers make me sick
And all these kids are waiting to sell the same mistakes as their own folks
I drive around this town, and in every abandoned building
Businesses that couldn't keep it together
I hear a voice from the inside of all that abandonment
It tells me to come inside
To forever lie among broken boards and dust long settled
Whatever this voice may be
It wants us all dead
Here
Just like the town we're dying in
Even in July, there's a whole lot of grey waiting to suck the color out of your
skin
I used to think if I drove around at night
When these fine middle-class Americans laid their minds at ease and slept,
The hours of this world between 10pm and 6am where there was only me,
I could escape them
But it just made the blood of this town that more evident
The loneliness is always more noticeable when there's even less to hate
You're surrounded by more of the same, but that's a different story
'Cause for now I drove around all night and never felt safe
In a town that will swallow your pride and spit you out sixty years older
With a bad back and a bed separated in two

You see
This town doesn't need to kill you by splitting your shine,
Shattering your skull,
Or impaling you in multiple places
There's no need for torture devices or ghosts that scare the color from your hair
You see,
This town would rather watch you wither away the little life you came here with
Streets grin as you to drive to places you hate
Fire trucks and cop cars wail their sirens in mocking laughter at another day gone dead
If traffic lights could reach down and strangle you
I am certain they would
But that ruins the beauty of watching you tie the noose, kick the chair and hang
While life out there goes on
Local obituary
Name:
Age:
Living relatives:
Job:
Length of residence:
And that is all your life would have meant
However many years beaten down between sports and finances
Maybe somebody who bought flowers from your boy-scout son
Will remember you over breakfast
They'll bring up your death casually
"Oh yeah, I do remember 'um. Damn shame."
Same thing they would have said about anybody else
Now from the obituary page
Withered down to one of five simple phrases from a pull-string doll
Today keeps getting better in good old Berkeley Heights, New Jersey
Sandwiched between two other shit towns
We just go around and around and around
Merry-Go-Nothing
The travesty of the middle class town
Is the local kid born who broke the mirror for seven years bad luck
Stayed here and decided to multiply that by ten
Now his gravestone cracks

While the town keeps dying
Whoring out lives for a laugh
"Hahahahahahahaha," said this miserable place.
'Hahahahahahahahaha!"

"Airplanes (Part 1)"

The world amazes me
So do people
Their towns, culture, and lives
Beautiful cities rise from the minds and hands of people only here for such a
short time
Answering all your little needs
But the unanswered, misunderstood concept of death still avoids us all
Nobody knows what it is, so we slapped a name on it and hoped for the best
I do the same with these words
Writing this is pointless when it won't get me any closer
If the only idea it pushes through my skull is to appreciate the beauty of the
now --
The lake behind my apartment,
A beautiful girl's smile,
The smell of a 6:30am Spring morning,
Driving off to a job so I can put food on my table --
Then let it be, and I'll lay low until the end brings me up to the end
When I swam as far down Death's door as possible and the current carried me
up
Sometimes faith feels like a leap between two ledges on crumbling mountains
Damned if I make it, damned if I don't
Either I fall long enough to realize what's happened
Or I crumble quickly among the stone that couldn't hold its place
My heart tells me that it ends and that's all s/he wrote
Then again, my heart steered me wrong many times before
Mainly when I told myself it was safe to bike down the top of a road
Correctly named "Skyline Dr."
And when I gave my brother the OK to jump off the roof into the pool
And he nearly impaled himself on the fence
Like some modern-day victim of Vlad the Impaler
I always associate death, God, religion, love, and my instincts
With these two childhood events
I laugh in its truth
I hide in the lies I create
But death always reminded me of an airplane
So far away from my eyesight and so full of figures, people and things
Going to places of an unknown destination to me
One, day Death will come down on me

Like an airplane diving
Like a city crumbling
Then I will know
All I'll have left behind is too many words proclaiming how little I understand
Maybe there is a God
Probably a fun son/daughter of a gun
Because he lets us one day learn the unknown parallels of Death
With no way of letting anybody else know
I can respect humor like that

"Painting the Crash Site (part 2)"

I pulled the trigger on nothing, and I was left with you
When the words became so untrue, I managed to lose that
You were replaced by four white walls that never talk
Just thick enough to hide all the outside sounds that would remind me
There was still life outside of what I created
I could paint them any color in the world and it still wouldn't bring anyone back
People seem to believe that being left alone is the easiest thing in the world
That it takes no effort to lose everything
Writing from the soul and spending all this time alone
Go hand in hand as well as writing in a crowded room
Alone or together, we're rotting ourselves out and not looking for the middle ground
Welcome to writer's block
Population: the captain and his anchor in a lake of fire
The fire set by others …fill my lungs
I cough out weak words and poor attempts to understand myself
Smother me out with a news report and your feelings on something you don't understand
I think I'd be better off burning in my own faults
Then again, that's how I got an intimate relationship
With four white walls that I haven't even decided what color I should paint them
If young kids playing with matches can start a forest fire
Big enough to take down the great wild
Think of what we could do if we only loved from a pure place
With a structure of encouraging others
Rather than being predisposed to recycling positive reinforcement
In favor of throwing out others hopes with the trash of our own misery
I'm left to pick it all up with a nod and a memory that I made up myself
A fantasy for what I wished for us
My god is a white wall that never blinks, talks back, balks, bleeds
Or lets the outside shine through
I pray with a scream and a reminisce
Of a time I could have sworn you walked through that wall
And back into the life I had let falter
I remember writing about death and a plane flying in the center of my face
Between the eyes slightly above the center of my nose

The place where all my problems begin
Mind explosion
It always comes back to a select few topics that I tried to disguise
Lies made beautiful
Yet no glue could piece together something with a weak structure and poor
foundation
I forced myself to write tonight
When I had the thought that no matter whom we sleep next to
And regardless of the last words we speak in an evening
We dream alone and only find rest for ourselves
I've embodied that outlook and all I was left with is this

"One Hit Wonder"

I'm a one-trick pony and this horse just kicked me in the throat
So I'm not focused on the now-thinning air
Just concerned if I'm a gimmick
Looking for a roadside show needing one more freak
Write me a check to break the bank
I'll owe you a penny for your thoughts
Broke or not, the thought that I am merely existing with no purpose is troubling
I greet the cold floor, missed meals and sleepless morning blues
As if they were the dear old friends I pretend they're not

"Sorry I could not be there tonight"

Blind and fruitless
The apple of no one's eye
I never heard the hissing of a snake wrapping itself around your sweetness
The beautiful inside
Not even those manmade devils in their farfetched stories
Want anything to do with your flesh peeling
If I ripped your memories apart
And tried to piece together the puzzle that was our dialogue
I would come up with a map leading to the outskirts of oblivion
Maybe we could wear it as a mask and see how long it would take
For the townspeople to throw stones and run us out of this place
It might be a favor they'd be doing us
They'd see me with a hint of disgust at the end of their tongue
The crust off the side of their mouth that they wipe off with broke hands
That would be me
Wearing what I tore off
Indifference
Not even that carries the weight it used to
In fact I think I could put it on my back and walk right out of town
That's where I plan on going
If I wear you or not
We've taken this as far as possible
Old Friend
Best friend
From here to the end
I'll carry this always

"Sayings"

I wish I could sing
But if wishes were fishes,
Something, something, something…
I never paid attention to the second half of that quote
Because it seemed I was always too busy being unable to get over what I
couldn't have
That was just fine
Holding on to the un-obtainable is the weak thing to do
And there is so much comfort in it
But that's not enough to give a good night's rest
You still fool yourself and scream that it's all you want
I've been where you stand, and I know it's a lie
Eyes deceive the mouth that springs the lies from souls held hostage
Good luck finding a gun strong enough
While I try and remember all the sayings you loaded into my head
Sit back and ready the firing squad of Hopelessness and Restlessness
Because yesterday I bought a used book on how to write
I found a message on the back
Directed at somebody named Kristina, from her parents
I felt like an intruder
"I know you're going to write something great one day. Happy birthday.
Love, Mom and Dad."
The fact that she ended up selling this book concerns me
I wonder if she ever wrote something great
I still don't know how to write
But the book looks well-loved
Edges broken down
The binding looking as if it's about to bust from its own stitching
Bar code sticker still in place
I wish I knew something about anything
Locked and loaded
I'd feel better if I could pop this and have my brain pour out something
useless
It's weather over here
Wish you were beautiful
But there's going to be a clean-up on aisle "Wasted Life"

"Time Is a Man Made Beast"

Your mother held you as a child and promised that time healed all wounds
But all time has done is decay
The end times won't be brimstone and hellfire
They'll show up slowly
Taking loved ones and lesser thans… slowly over the years
Our lives, the insignificant breath
The world lets us create our own god in the form of naming things
Creating time
'Cause sweetheart, baby girl, Miss
If we lived forever
Eventually there'd be nothing
This world survived before us and once we came
It found a way to let us
So waiting for time to heal is to wait in your bed
Anticipating your heartbeat slowing down to a soundless sunset
There's no rhythm in nothing
We sink this world to shit
And eat around its wound
Act surprised when we die and raise our own to do more of the same

"How can we know anything?"

I can't tell if the above is the name of a poem in line
Or a question looking for a logical answer
How can I be sure if this life I'm living is really fit for me?
Or any other man searching for something to love and reach for
Are my goals reachable, or just another section of my life
Filled with new problems to write the same ol' poem with?
The books I find, the information I have come to accept
I wait for the day I reach for my door and the sun shines falsehoods right into
my kitchen
Looking like the intro to some orange juice commercial
Instead the fruit's rotting and the glass is half empty
But what's left in the bottom of the mug is foul
And all the wrongs I thought were rights in darker colors
Will write messages of truth
Like I'm the modern day Jesus about to sit down for the last breakfast
But if this moment because a famous picture
There'd be no best friend Judas or people begging to me in the middle of
delights
I'd be sitting by myself and reading a new reality that shows
Wasted years, crossed out peers and relationships
As the rotten junk in the pit of my stomach
So how do dreams work? Where is their master?
Why are there books on such, and how do you know
A dream of me eating an apple with dead presidents
Is a subconscious message that I really hate my father?
Cause I've been dreamin' of cheatin' and runnin' from these ghosts
I've been wakin' up with headaches and a dry mouth
After sinkin' in sand in the middle of a dessert with nobody around
Wondering how I could have just been in my childhood home
Maybe there is more to this than I originally thought
Have you ever sat and wondered if this universe is really just a blade of grass
In a much bigger universe, two inches from the lawnmower ready to run us
down?
Mow us to nothing
The great end for us
May just be a wasted weekend of a wife yelling at her husband to cut the grass

What means everything to us may be nothing in a big picture we will never
see
Our eyes are not wide enough to see the whole frame,
Nor do we have the knowledge of all the colors involved
Wouldn't that be something to find out we're all nothing?

"All These Things Fight For Me"

I write this with a hesitation great enough to grow May flowers
Before their April showers
There's a part of me that wonders, though
A wonder that grows until I'm concerned if I think about it anymore,
It will spill out of every orifice in my body and imprison me wherever I sit
To leave me to think about it forever
So with one final plea of wasted time, I digress
What if our morals played a much more simple game with us?
Instead of Armageddon with flaming stones
Crashing down on innocent bystanders and Devil advocates alike
The greatest scam of all
That I think the God and Devil were both in on
Maybe our lives aren't decided by abortions and marriage,
But rather the simple kindness to strangers
And our own interpersonal ability to wash away the lingering aftertaste
Of bitterness towards our loved ones and enemies
As if we saw them for how similar they really are
This frightens me beyond recognition
If that's the case, I'm one death away
From being found guilty of the charges of petty aggression
I'm a pathetic dog limping across a highway
Hoping I won't find a love story end with the front bumper of Kansas or
Oregon truck
Some far off land
I don't want to die without riding this ship in the storm
To have my guts lie out on the street for everyone to see
Just because I couldn't get over myself
Long enough to not flip off the guy who just cut me off
The misplaced aggression connects you and I
As my arms are ripping at the seams
Angel wings weave with devil horns and other manmade folklore
While I can't even properly place my own feelings
This confession feels empty and pointless, but the point still stands
Even if I am having trouble finding my own balance

"The Alphabet Poem"

A.

I avoided writing this like the plague
So look at me and realize I came down with this illness anyway
I remember wishing I could be more like you
Before I realized life isn't a one-size-fits-all
It's a personalized domain of insecurity and scars
How beautiful
I feel bad you'll never see it, but I won't feel guilt
I let that emotion make a coward of this vessel for far too long
It held grip of my hand as I opened up doors that walked over everything I
had to say
Footprints guided me from one destination to another
Naïve and easily influenced
I hate to look at what used to be
Even now that I know the good that came from it
We locked eyes when I was nothing
Now we avoid the stare when we became everything
What a disappointing end
Living through the war to die malnourished in the epilogue
You now haunt me, prologue
Only because I know where you'll go
If I had one wish in the palms I sink my face into
It would be to warn you
But then I'd lose what I have left
Leading me to believe that "everything" and "nothing"
Are the most unproductive words created
Reaching for both ends of the stick that burnt off
Not even the embers that scar can take us away
I'll see you again in certain parts
I'll mourn you in the ones you're no longer in

B.

Behind every great thief is a once promising child
The only things quicker than your hands
Are the broken wounds that rot out the bigger picture
The frame given to you, now in shambles
While you're stealing a golden one for the smile you'd love for people to
believe
It still looks ever so crooked in the palace of gimmicks
Sell what you steal when you can't buy what you lost
One of the few things you need
Fill up rooms of juvenile longing
It won't make them seem less empty
Storms thrive in places like this
They see what others are too selfish to look for
Weak floorboards built by weaker minds
You think you can steal everything but your sanity
There's a convincing argument, though, when you're falling asleep
That there is a part of your soul that defies gravity
And sinks upwards into your throat
Falling right into the part of you that hasn't learned to cheat yourself
Showing you how shallow this path really is
The last thought you have of the night that leads into nightmares:
You can have the most beautiful casket ever built
Doesn't really matter if nobody worth their weight in morals is there to bury
you
They'll just steal what they can from you
By then it's too late
Worse though…
Nobody will have bothered to stick around
To find out what you thought when you died
The person most important, the one that flashed themself to you before you
passed
Beggars realize the rivers dried up before the townspeople are even thirsty
Deep down that's all you'll ever be
So this shouldn't come as a surprise
But I am sure you'll pretend

C.

You are all I want when I'm sick
The only arms I want to hold me when I'm disgusted with my face
When the look of me laughs back
As soon as my eyes droop down past my hanging head
I know your hands will pull me back to this world
You're in everything I write
Even when it's about what you wish I wouldn't write about
I look back and see how far I've come, and I am afraid
There is a belief somewhere I wish I could throw off the face of the earth
That tells me (or lies to me)
That I haven't come half as far as I'd like everybody to believe
That it is only because I have gripped into you and made you pull me up
alongside you
The ever-growing fear that I am nothing but a bitter preacher of nothing
without you
The screaming child begging for the ground he's not ready to walk on yet
Just too stubborn to even understand that
You are everything at the peak of creativity
Same as you are when morale is at its lowest
The one steady ship I was allowed to become a part of
When I was abandoned at sea
Regardless of everything else
I lay my head and know the difference between the home I was given
And the one I've made with you

D.

I get the sneaking thought
That this world is jealous of everything you could be
Loving the fatigue that feels unavoidable
The one that turns into years of pent-up denial and regret that keeps building
In the lay of your land
That's how the world wants you to feel
Their love is found in making those above and beyond them
Feel lower than the lowest of them
Yet I hope you still believe in the fact
That lesser eyes can't penetrate the mind that lets itself feel everything
Even when it's enough to make you want to throw it all away
You care too much
What a beautiful thought that isn't sung enough in this day and age
I have to tell you something
Right here and now
You will die one day
So will I
Everyone you've known and loved will one day be wiped away from here
There may be a horrific moment in time where you will pick up the phone to
call
And share a small moment of your day with somebody you love
A person you confide in
You won't be able to
They will be dead
And in a mere emotional crutch of a reflex
You still reached out for arms you wished were alive
There are inevitable moments in life where our own devils take hold
And we engulf in the flame of self-loathing
We'll sink in the never-ending despair of time we wasted with loved ones now
gone
If I don't laugh at how simple this is, I would cry myself insane
We're here, and then we won't be
I may be writing to you right now but I'm not penning this for you
It's just a reminder to me
To bite my tongue and love this life
Enjoying the comfort and short phone calls of those in it
Small memories in time that take on more weight
As days turn calendars throughout the years

I know this is hard
But it's all there is.
It's beautiful.
Everything.
Always.
Yet not forever.
I hope when you read this, it is still in the now
You hold such beauty in your hands and you don't even understand
Open your eyes
Keep your hands not like a prison
Do not crush what is in front of you
One day it make just be a crack in the road
One you can't see
The only place you may want to be in the future
Is where you are now.

E.

This one stands for what I felt was missing
The name I spent my life trying to outrun
I just kick up dirt that isn't married to the ground
Exhale it in a new direction
The wind will make sure it doesn't stay long
You can line up a bunch of lifeless people
Who wish their legs ran as fast as their judgment
And the one idea I keep coming back to in this poem, this idea
Is that what we're running from is maybe where we should be
It's not trying to rip us to pieces
It just wants to pick up what we left
What we felt was ugly or unimportant
It is the great unknown and that is okay
Because it is what we make it
I wanted to be afraid so I never let my thoughts-turned-ghosts
Entertain the idea of becoming a part of my life again
The poison it boiled up should have ended me twenty times over
The repetition I've found is only matched by how much it was deserved
I used to feel so distraught with who I was and the people who had to
tolerate it
Until I learned from it
And stopped running
Only then when I allowed myself to simply take a moment to just be
Did I truly understand how much wrong I had let creep in
How easy the darkened path is to find
The light at the entrance dies there
Because it's so hard to find anything
When you've gone too far into your own inferiority complex
That's all it ever was
I remember someone I loved stared me dead in the eyes so fast,
I thought I was a goner
Let me know that she had never met anybody who seemed so disgusted with
the world
I was young and felt that with a sliver of pride
That is now the only thing I feel disgusted about
How naïve I am in feeling so small
There is no purity in hate

Knowledge won't find a nest in venom spat out at innocence
E is for empty
For everything that I was
When I wouldn't let you near
Or how much I really did care

F.

This is the word of loss
Written from hard luck in our despair
The broken heart that seems to find every penny tails-up in the ground
When they're face down in their own mind games that they can't ever seem to
win
We're really only playing ourselves
So when we cheat, who are we really beating?
Answerless questions are made into essays
My pencil just broke
The dog ate my homework
Grandma broke her hip
And I lost the doctor's note I had on my way here, I swear
All excuses I make up when I'm running to the well of good words
And I'm coming up with desert sand; it's slipping beneath my fingers
Hoping to find a different path
It just leaves me with the reminiscent dust on my hands
Right now they're out of control
Sign language of foul F words
The grade I got
Failure
Fraud
Fuck-up
Fall
Flat
Forgotten
Frail
Take your pick while I'm picking my fingernails off my hands
To try and get them to stop
I don't speak the language
Yet I do, however, speak the urgency
I understand that
The feeling in the heart
The sweat on the forehead and the eyes gazing everywhere at once
What a crazy thought
The one I often feel
If words are all I have and I can speak a million words but the one I love
Then I'm the world's worst thief
Pick-pocketing myself

Always surprised when I find the coin face down
The definition of insanity
When I'm weak and trying to give up
I pretend I'm the definition for a lot of words I shouldn't speak
With my mind, eyes or hands
Vocal pitch or other audio or body language I may have missed
For I am learning that self-loathing and the disgust that falls out of it
Is merely a denial in the art of learning from one's mistakes
And I have a gallery full of them

G.

So if I'm a poor man's version of my own illusion
Am I begging for change or an outlet?
I know there is something better inside
But with a schedule full of looking outward
At a window two inches away from a brick wall
Clearly I am busy in a staring contest with nothing
The something I know won't make me question
Any of the things I have asked of myself
Not the something I need though
Just the easy one to want
The bricks I'm trying to break with eye contact
Are the ones I need to break away from
But I'm breaking my toes
So I don't have to break from this continuing habit of insanity
I have lost the ambition to proclaim importance on what potential you had
Not to myself but everybody else
I no longer wanted to keep you bottled up for myself
Like a bad drinking habit that feels there has to be one bottle
Where instead of headaches and bad life breaks
There may be a message
With an idea
Sparking some great fury that Hell couldn't hold
And Heaven wouldn't have the guts to glorify
In fact there is none
No what?
Exactly
There may be nothing among the blossoming goals of your life
I'm breaking myself as I try and destroy what I built
The idea of prison was always so interesting to me
It's not makeshift weapons and sunlight lost among cold concrete
With unforgiving metals trying to keep men from their hope
It is, however, the limitations I have given to myself
I refrain from saying "you" and replace it with "I"
Because maybe I really am alone
Insane
Hiding under walls marked with words to justify the repetition of such foul
habits
I clench my teeth like I'm looking to imprison my tongue

Keep it from your ear
You
The all-knowing
Turned into the "never ever"
Even "after" was happily ended
Among words running out
While they're trying to run free of the cell they created
No matter what breaks my feet may catch,
The one thing I'll never outrun is myself
Not even if the cracks I fear become the life I lost
And break myself into pieces
Small, watered-down ideas that harden themselves
Back into the reconstruction of a prison
That I thought of breaking out of
When I was blocking out the sun
With the brick of insecurity
Cemented by fear
On the ground of isolation
Of the self
From the self and for
The all-knowing within
Wasting away inside of itself

H.

I see fragments of my mistakes in everyone around me
Causing my stomach to churn
Almost as if I was turning myself inside out from the guilt inside the grief
Built into its shell of mishaps and regrets
There's a part of my brain that throbs with anxiety
At the idea of going out at times

That was all I wanted to write here
Yet as I sat back and thought of the first word that came to mind
When I saw the letter H
The answer was hanging
Hanging out the window of my own life
Ready to jump
To release my own thoughts and sacrifice my bones back in which I came
Leave behind nothing but the world to digest my bones to brittleness before
dust
I also thought of hanging from a tree that didn't break my neck
The tree
Every branch, every piece of bark to the highest leaves on this tree
To its deepest root buried within the dirt
Each individual part of this tree was made up of my wrongdoings
My guilt and my foolishness
Swaying back and forth
With nothing on my schedule but being faced with having to look at it
From every degree and corner
When there is nothing but you,
Your mistakes,
And time between you dictating how you think,
You learn to give up petty terms and excuses
Being naïve
Not knowing the difference
What's the point in lying when there's nothing left in your life but the truth?
Often, I feel withdrawn
More so than that, I feel guilty about that
It's not you that made me feel this way
It must be the small part of my mind
That I tuck away all the things that I pretend don't exist
What makes it worse is I don't know if I'm wrong or right

Worse than all
I don't know what I am to you
So to all the lost poets
The morally astray, who are halfway through life's journey
Pass by me
Rip the bark from my tree
Watch me bleed
Cup my choices into your hand
And drink from the body of regret
Before you move on to the mistakes of others
I wonder if you'll learn from mine
I even wonder if there's still time for me
The noose is loose and the rope is burning brightly
Yet all I worry about is the fall
The least of my worries is what I spend the most time on
That's my mental catchphrase
I end this with no comfort because I have yet to decide
If these words are an apology are not
Jaded or hard-headed?
Nostalgic or bitter?
With a rope burning at both ends I'm running out of time

I.

Impressing the impersonal
Unimpressed with the worshipping of flesh servants for a green god
That strikes down the majority when the large imagination won't fit
In the slim binding suit of a snake with dollar sign eyes and a suit made of
coin scales
Gripping the life out of the creative
Governed by the self
If that's the metaphor, then the reality is
I'm choked up on pressure points that hits me right in the heart
Filtered through how it felt in my mind
With eyes lying about what's two inches in front of my face
Killing ants with atomic bombs
Decapitating to spite the lacerations across the cheek
Scarred and guarded are too many in these days
Where we put faith into the right now when we're living in a final today
Monday morning water cooler conversations
Have caused us to avoid the states of our emotional degradation
When I say I
I think of all the opinions of you
So all the letters before, after, and in between fly right here
To try and save myself
But it's a mission so foolish for someone not wise enough to take under
The raindrop looking for the rhythm in the rain
Before I explode onto a surface and coagulate in pieces of my brothers
The many make the flood
And the single gets wiped away by windshield wipers
On a highway to nowhere
From the workplace of the emotional beaten slave
Wiped by wisecracks, sharp words, and passive-aggressive adjectives
In ell they live
Fire reigns un-obtained or un-ignited by a single raindrop
Trying to flood the gates of Hades
In ways, those previous seem undesired
By the rhythm-lacking water drops in the storm
Two left feet and not a beat between
I am unseen in the storm
You have weaned me of personal, alluring fragrance of content
Dry desert, hell bent

The creative flow
Damned up by corruption
Never known by the peers
Never seen by me
Never felt by you
When it's all strangled out
In a storm trying to put out an all-consuming hate
Breaking down an undying love

J

Assuring you that it's all going to be okay
Is like carrying the dead on your back everywhere you go
For me writing isn't as simple as
Roses are red
Violets are blue
Because there's such a weakness inside of me
I'm not even worthy of describing what you think is beautiful
If I could forget a large chunk of my life
I'd bite it off the throat of beauty and spit into it the mouth of anger
That's how I feel when I wake up from a dream that didn't even involve me
From the eyes of others I see the wrongs in me
Bleeding with the wrongs of yours
My disappointment is red
Your disapproval is violet
Together I'm painting ugly portraits with a purplish red
They're dripping off the canvas
Trying to escape the brush and leave the home of the page
Because they want no part in this loathing
So now I have this weird pink puddle at my feet I could drown my woes in
Yet they're more of a reminder than what I tried to express
Puddles of paint can't speak
Canvases can't scream
And colors are just colors
So it all comes back
The meaning I give to the most mundane of things on the dullest of days
Afternoons spent wanting everything to be so different
So here's a confession:
All I want is to be alone and forget
Because there's a huge part of me I would love to let go
Drown it in the sea
Burn it in the fire
Whatever
Whenever
Life's short and pride is in low supply
Just ask my eyes and the way they never look up at the sky
Instead of digging for the reason
It's easy to get lost in the cause
I only confess to this page

If I went to your church to do so, I'd get lost in your steeple
Fall in lust with the beauty of your bell now ringing
Live in the sound they make
Forget all about the reason I am here
Afraid to love yourself
It just results in hatred misplaced
Look for it in a lost and found that's been abandoned
Ring the bell at the desk
Just to remind yourself of church bells in the distance
The sound in your seduction
The heart on my tongue bounces off the lips that slips you lies and misdirect
If one has to try and justify the reason
They've spent little to no time asking why

K.

If words that rhymed made this beautiful enough for you to find
I would memorize dictionaries searching for words that, when combined,
Could express my thoughts
I would train my voice to make awkward phrases whip out of my mouth
With ease and intensities
The language in which I spoke would have to do whatever my pen said
If killing with kindness could bring it all back
I'd be on a murder spree to the umpteenth degree
Holding doors open for those I've never known and greeting every passing
glare
With a smile and a "I hope today brings you everything you want and need"
If I could breed a better truth through your ears
And kiss your mind with my emotions
I'd walk old ladies across the street until I wore my feet down into bloody
stumps
Even though I'd drag myself via tooth and nail
If it would result in leading me inches closer
To a grace that I thought could save
However --
And I hate to use that word --
I am learning that relief only hits you
When you shoot yourself with clarity between your eyes
So much is within, and I'm a disgrace to my own savior
The self
When I hold my hands out instead of using them to dig deeper
Into the bigger problem of me
The one. The self. The only being I will truly ever know.
The only one I don't sing for
Because I choked all of my songbirds on the feathers of the others
Now I'm just left wingless and without a voice
While you're off singing in the clouds

L.

Leave Love how you found it
Lone
The trifecta of Loss
Hello father, have you found the Holy Ghost?
Because I, the Son, am so ready to give myself out for the greater cause
That Keats and co. told me was so worth leaving this world for
Bathed in misfortune
Down a drain I'm thinking I'd be better off, if I could crawl down
Swimming around like the records that inspired people just like you
The ones I wish I had written
But I haven't invested in writing utensils lately
Because I have had no hunger to feed
Starve myself for no greater good than a scoff and a passing laugh
Worlds crash for this word
Wars start from the loss
When burning desires turned to hellfire snowed over
Bury me where the snow falls over the last memory I have
A coma for my conscience when I'm all out of pennies for thoughts
I could drown in your fountain
If you're chiseled from perfection
I was smashed in from imperfections glued together
Chipped and worn when words leave to loathing
A lifetime scorned
The Abortion
Reborn
The only word the world every blessed me with was a curse
Love
All knowing perfection that is ever misleading
If there's no God laughing down with this brilliant sense of humor
Then people are the funniest accidents to ever happen
Laughing to death at the original crash site
Visionless
Blind
Love is the worst seeing-eye dog a man could find
Guiding you to make sweet grace with oncoming traffic
If I was an artist I'd have drawn a picture of war on the battlefield of my
forehead
With the sweat you've made me pour out of myself

Yet I am just another science experiment trying to find my cage
To rip through
Even though I'd rather sty here and capture
The all-knowing and ever so consumed beautiful ugliness of a word
That has lead to everything

M.

Moon and Sun
The day and the night follow each other like naïve love-struck fools
Still I fail myself
With the prospect of even the most simple and heartfelt ideas
To be honest, I still hate the rain
But that doesn't seem to stop it from trying to wipe my slate away
Clean seems like a far-off distant word for something that is now
indescribable
Not when, for the first time, I'm seeing blind fools of my yesteryears
Lying to one another and trying to sell happiness
I never thought I would ask for the feeling of guilt to tug on my shoulder
When I was turning around
Yet here I am, wishing your absence could conjure up some kind of emotion
in me
Negative or not
When you're no longer here or there
I have come to accept you for what you are
While I was looking in to find the growth I desperately needed
I confess now that when I last saw you
There was nothing to talk about
Worst of all, I knew that you felt the same
What a horrific finale
When those that used to be so close
Can't even find a moment to be honest
To say the one thing that not even their eyes can lie about
I am gutless when I am lying to myself
To save something that has been dead a good while
Once so naïve
The truth isn't so sweet these days
Certain moments used to mean so much
Now they're simply a time
A place
During a night
That held a group of people
A moment I now look at with a distance that is too far to let me get a good
look
Maybe I've lost clarity
Not even that feels like a good enough lie

Every single time I've written the word "maybe" was because
I wanted to hide from the truth
Like the gutless coward I showed you
A reflection of each other
I had a chance to see you today
A moment in time I could catch
I let this become a memory that I watched shatter
I picked up the pieces and I didn't feel a thing

N.

Our time together was compiled into a movie reel
Each sequence played out a little more distressed with each inch
Until it caught fire before I had to live with it for another moment
The last thing I saw
Was a pair of hands reaching
And the pains of hearing "no"
That is what I'll remember most
The only thing I will actually take away
That one singular event engulfed every other moment I can remember
Burning it away
Could you imagine?
If we could recount every memory we lived?
All the conversations we've had?
Ignorance is bliss
And I found heaven in forgetting you
My only regret that I find in the lesser part of my most petty of traits
Is that I couldn't give you everything you wish you had
Just to watch you come to the conclusion that you're even more alone than
you thought
The bullshit spewed from the furnace found its way to the bottom of hell
Here or there, when or where
All small scenes in the production of your tragedy with no real substance
I was a minor character with a role that played itself out
You said no to nothing
Then fell to your knees with surprise
Like you couldn't see it coming

O.

My opinions were set in stone before the rock even grew from the earth's crust
A defense mechanism for cowards
The word I tried to distance myself
The outsider I now feel like, in a kingdom with rotting thrones
I promised myself better, but my insecurities ate me alive
Now I'm writing this from the stomach of disgruntled anger
I slipped right down the throat of fear
After the lips of ill thought caressed me into believing
I wouldn't be digested by my own mistakes
Yet here I am
Another number in a collection of billions
You could leave my grave unmarked, and it wouldn't matter much
Old is the word that cues the laughter in the stomach of the young
Yet it is the world that sends chills down my back so strong
My fingertips fears the earthquake growing inside nervous smirks
In a crowded room in which I lay unknown
The greatest of my fears, born again with even less reason
Self -induced failure is the cancer of creativity
Once again, fear grips me tight and whispers that I am the latest of lost cases
Then I realize I am alone
And talking myself all the way into that unmarked grave
"Bury yourself in cement," said self-destruction.
"I don't want there to be any chance of a resurrection."
Rebirth is the only word they fear
It is now the only thing that matters to me
The one word I will truly know
As it plays out before the eyes of the earth I walk

P.

The idea of death can be suffocating. I feel it grabbing me by the throat and trying to cut off my air supply. I'd like to believe an explanation that melodramatic, but the truth is I am scaring myself. It is the fear of being unable to accomplish anything worth remembering to those who I feel so uncomfortable being in the same room with. It is a cycle that I would love to call vicious, but I feel that's the coward's way out.

I sit most uncomfortably among my shortcomings, because I treat them as if everybody around me can see them. This gives way to phobias that vomit fear and anger upon itself. In fact, I don't think it's vicious. It's self-destructive. I'd rather pretend the jaws ripping my life to shreds don't come from my own mouth, but I have spit in the face of this world in the worst possible way, of not living it to the full extent.

The fact that I have entertained the idea of letting my mind collapse upon action and reason shames me into even further regression. You were always the one who told me I could make it; this statement scared me, and I resented you for being honest when everybody else turned away from me. I thought myself so ugly, I thought only a fool could see beauty in my mistakes. I wanted to alienate you, say something horrific to watch you flinch because of how much I had begun to question my own reason. You told the truth and I cast you out for it. I have no excuse but admitting that the ugliest side of me was not listening to you self-disclose over the beauty of life.

On the outside, I met you and thought I was a man, but now I feel like an exposed child, vulnerable to the harsh nature of this world. Looking back, I remember the innocence and good intent of all your help. Even more so, I remember looking at you and wanting to see blood, to say something so horrific you'd run away forever, just so I could go back to being an insecure child.

I started this at one point and ended up at another; that happens often when I try to hide my truth in the wrongs I stand by. I feel the earth shattering below me, and I remember your face. I believe that the weakest of human beings only realize their true beauty and potential right before they die, if they're even lucky enough to see it coming, for there is a legion of tales that comes from a screen that tells me of all the ends of life that happened in a moment. In one second, everything that once was is now something that can never again be as it was. This in itself distresses me more so than anything. Yet, to be such a coward that I only saw everything that was beautiful as it is being stripped from me is the most humiliating end of all.

I hope you can forgive for taking this long to write this for you and admit to myself in this confessional, what you've begged me to verbalize for so long. This is my first attempt at fearlessly reaching for things that may not reach back. To live in a moment of loss, isolation, sadness, and rejection is the first step in truly being alive.

Q.

It is Friday night, and I am alone. The humidity clings to my skin just enough to make me feel filthy. Wind chimes and the sound of my heels against the pavement are my only soundtracks, with the occasional interlude of cars going too fast on a twenty-five mile per hour road and the ever-so-enthusiastic patrons of the car yelling at me or honking as they go on to what, in their minds, will be a fulfilling night of entertainment.

They are in my life and out in a moment of seconds, and I feel all the more empty. I question if I belong and if anyone can see it. I feel like a shadow of a formally socially acceptable self that now horrifies me. If happiness holds hands with ignorance, I'll go screaming into a silent night limbless. A siren goes off in the distance, as the sound of wind chimes dims at my back. I wonder the nature of the call: drunk driving, domestic dispute, robbery, etc., etc. I feel lost in a never-ending garbage dump. Rancid smells fill my nostrils while the sight of it all is even less appetizing.

Every moment, it all dims, and all the lines blur. My sense of smell is desensitized to the rank scent of passive behavior in the face of immoral behavior. With blindness, I imagine myself feeling around my surroundings to a better paradise, yet in the process, I have dirtied my hands beyond recognition. Now I will be blind with the dirt and blood of all I have grown to detest on me as well, this all on the stage of a never-ending search for lesser people in humanity.

There comes a time in every human being's life, where they can either rise above what they've been given and risk martyrdom and loneliness, or sink to social glory with their peers laughing into the abyss of which we know nothing about. I bring this isolation upon myself. I write this not in loathing but in acknowledgment, to loosen its grip over my heart and admit to myself the fear of the unknown. This is merely recognition, not a melodramatic plea to eyes bouncing from left to right. I ruin myself by looking outward and seeing smiling faces that once looked familiar. I don't understand most of what I love. The idea that I loved a mirage of the truth or an idea that I wished into existence is as horrific as it is liberating. Looking for peace of mind in the eyes, minds, and arms of others is like seeking warmth in the snow during a blizzard, and all I see are frozen fragments of what I used to know.

My fingerprints kissed the cold years gone by, and they shattered, letting me see myself in several broken images, leading to no road in particular. Still, even with this, my only soundtrack is far off wind chimes to the back of my neck and the rhythmic stomp of my heels against a pavement I'm waiting on to crack. These are the thoughts I am now left with, as another unknown passes me by, to some destination, searching for something.

R.

I question the motives of my closest confidantes and expect the worst from perfect strangers. If I awoke tomorrow and found that humanity had allowed the selfish and animalistic needs of the faux self righteous to bowl its way out of their minds, I wouldn't even question it. We are all holding on by such a small rope that if we took the time to think about it, we'd simply let go and fall for a good long time.

These thoughts seize the innards of my vocal chords and squeeze. They grip all entry points for anxiety and hold them captive. I am left with feeling tiresome and the disappointment that I have allowed myself to regress as a human being. This is not what I expect from myself, yet it has become so easy to expect the worst with such ease, you'd almost think I wanted it that way. At the bottom of these thoughts I feel small and afraid. Yet I have dug a grave so deep and become so close to the dirt I ascended from, I don't remember the original point or why I have caked myself with filth in the process.

I threw a stone down the grave of my insecurity and waited for the echo of rock bottom and all I did was wait. Life is beautiful, but as we progress, our minds become a graveyard full of buried thoughts and repressed memories that we cremated and spread over the ocean that is the outskirts of our own infinity. Cracked tombstones let ourselves know of the wear and tear effect this world will have on the mind in one lifetime. The idea of living becomes blurred, when all I do is spend the most valuable of time burying the lowest of past feelings.

Am I my own caretaker, or just a dead memory that lost its grave? The time spent here has allowed me to get lost in the shadows of what could have been. I let my eyes adapt, and I waited while making excuses for not scratching the dirt off my hands. This isn't living, it's just patiently waiting for the right moment to give in and go home to a place that no longer exists.

There was once a time where I believed in us and core values that we preached. Now it has come to the surface that they were as empty as the graves I dig up, searching for meaning, for anything at all. Waiting and regressing are the two destinations, and I am their prisoner in the middle, like the pendulum that holds our time at the end, like the prisoner watching the blade swing, from one to another, until it is low enough in the middle to take away what I haven't earned or upheld the privilege of calling my own.

S.

There are certain things in which I find it increasingly difficult to be honest with myself, a certain degree of separation that is necessary for me to keep from others and myself. There are scars that must be left unknown to even the greatest of people whom I have had the pleasure of knowing and learning from, especially now when I look back in retrospect at a time where I played along, sang their songs, and listened to their reasoning.

I fooled myself into feeling good, if even for the moment. I was a fraud, and a part of me still is for missing it. Fate is a topic I rarely think of, but if it is indeed a real metaphysical aspect of our lives, it watched me those thousand and some days and must have nodded its head, knowing I would one day come back to the life I would lead. Thank you for giving me the opportunity to sleep at night without thoughts of disillusion to fill my skull.

However, I strongly believe that a small part of my being was fully aware of the clock that was counting down on my part on this play. My feet plague their skin with splinters from a stage that is so desperate to throw me off that it is destroying itself. Infiltrating my thought process with the idea of returning brings along with it a headless horseman of anxiety who swings at strangers, the simple idea that it can have company if they take away the sight and sound of everybody else. In doing this, I have hurt myself and most around me, apologizing to no one in particular.

An anonymous page will do nothing for anybody. The only thing is, it leaves me to wonder if the only reason I regret this is because it is the knowledge that one day will be our last. There will be a day before our deaths in which we think about each other for the last time, and even if we know we're dying, it is hard to predict the last time the entity that is you will inflict my soul. It will bury me deeper than the scars and thoughts I wish to keep from everything I loved or once thought I did. It could very well be a moment of mourning a person I will never see again as I fade away in some bed, knowing that the possibility I am feeling things for the last time is upon me. Or a candid moment as I cross the street as a healthy person before a drunk driver breaks my back and crushes organs in the wake of his own horrific behavior.

I don't believe in the concept of waking to a day I will not see the end of, or regretting not taking a fraction of time from petty annoyances to enjoy the beautiful surroundings I have been granted. I believe that the last time I think of you, yes you, will be filled with anger, and a fear that there was not enough effort in caring about you expressed in my actions. I have been selfish and did it for my own reasons so much, that the ugliest parts of me were an unlovable mess of panic, anxiety, and culture crashing down on my chest.

These are not excuses, they are merely an expression of a thought I had one night, in which I feared the last time each other's names would grace the vast and perfect plain that is our minds. If I apologize for anything here, let it be for the fact that I confessed here and not directly, that I have expressed these scars in a vague and bipolar manner. There is nothing perfect about us but the beautiful land we've been placed in. I don't know if any of you will ever read this, or even approve, and I doubt it will ease me into sleep any better tonight, but it is now here. I hope that this is not the last time for anything, for all of you.

T.

Tonight there was a television program that featured a singer performing in an American flag dress. Behind her were male dancers dressed in army fatigues. There was a large crowd who seem mesmerized by the performance and the fireworks exploding behind the performers. I thought of my friends in the military and their horror stories. An image arose in my mind of a nameless solder dying alone on the battlefield, scared and miles away from his family. I assumed they wouldn't mention any horror stories on that stage, or show any concern for people who fought and died so she can look stupid on that stage, belittling outfit and all.

I am not political, nor do the events that play out in front of my television arouse any words of faith in one political ideal or another. I just can't help but shake my head, resting on lowered shoulders, at the idea that we pretend like we spend calendar-marked days of smiley faces by drinking ourselves into a trance or only finding joy in what we're doing. We ironically celebrate our independence by being dependent on spoon-fed nonsense.

Real beauty can appear ugly on the surface, and we ignore it all for no better tomorrow. I feel for the ugliest beauty who isn't allowed to spread the gift of knowledge and experience because they're not formatted for financial gain. The beauty of life will teach you the greatest things when you are at your worst. You see the stage and the performance, but they won't allow you to watch the wood splinter as the foundation comes crashing. The dust settles around the hope of a better day and stays there forever. There are so many lies being dressed up for skin-deep novelty.

We accept the entanglement and trivial behaviors as groundbreaking because they are followed by a trail of man made paper. This paves over the ugliness that the world hides from you, the horror spoken of as if it were dinner conversation. This world leaves me afraid when thoughts like these cross my head.

To the nameless dead and the inescapably isolated, I am sorry all the lessons you could have taught have been suffocated under the rug they swept you under. This haunts me at every turn, and I will give a moment to you when I lay awake in bed tonight. The fan soothes my need for sound as I hope for a better day not in sight, while I lay in a blinded night, with a far off dawn.

U.

This morning, there is a beautiful and tranquil calm that has seemingly taken over the landscape. I embrace it with such a great hesitation. I take in air and moments alike with a reserve meant for only the most doubtful part of my mind. I walk on petty discontent like it means something. If I knew what little weight this truly held, I might just fall forever. My own subconscious and belittled fears will be the walls I see only in spats and blurs, as I dive face-first into a fire that I always feel but never quite reach. I walk this far enough, until I reach a meaningless morning task that I can't afford to quit but refuse to let go.

There is age all around me now. Knowledge, warning signs, and fear. A bleak outlook eclipses itself over the faces of those around me. Tales are spoken of with a quiet nervousness on the bags under their eyes. Tired eyes and regretful minds, they are the only future held here. I feel the subtle anger under your breath as you give me mindless tasks. There is a terror that strikes the core of the chest at passive aggressive smirks, snorts, and back talk. I feel pettiness all around me, inside of me. Those same verbal jabs find birth in my mind and are born right out of my mouth. The beginning stages of the roots digging my feet into the soil of self-hatred have begun.

So many around me stand idle in this state and wait for the sweet relief of denial to wash over them, yet I wish to drown myself for an answer. The antithesis to the anchor that runs circles around me, No metaphor could make me comfortable enough to truly talk about this. I sit here, unaware of the weather and all I can think is, "Why the fuck have I not written anything funny and clever here?"

I look at my peers and I doubt myself for not cleverly making an analogy to make someone chuckle. Pettiness has found me, depleted confidence narc'ed on me, and now I'm running in the sea, with anchors on my feet while falling through hellfire. Maybe I was wrong, maybe this is funny, and the joke of you, has infected the I.

Terminally, your aborted dreams
With all the love in the world

V.

The world digs us up one grave at a time, and it's beating down my casket. It all started when I formed an agnostic relationship with virtue, while absent friends hung from empty nooses on rotten branches. I am left with the greatest ally named Change, yet often it is dressed as an enemy and has to take me kicking and screaming.

I feel so utterly uncomfortable around you that I can't even look at the faces of old photographs anymore. I dread the idea of having to spend even a moment in the same room as you. Dreadful silence would creep up on us and I would allow this to run rampant in my mind. I am not a victim, nor do I cry out words of injustice. Yet there will never be a moment where I comprehend how saying I would die for you and all the others would end up being the death of me.

Thoughts of you arise in my mind and I am taken back to times of comfort and understanding until the reality of time and what it has taken blankets over the fire, leaving these thoughts to inhale the dying smoke to a once beautiful flame.

W.

In this moment, I am hit with a monumental wave that finds safety in my lungs. It was strung together from a great above with a harrowing mix of nostalgia, fear, regret, and a reluctant confession that there are moments in time I should have appreciated more. The task of propelling myself through memories and realizing all of the petty and insignificant moments that plagued a healthy home grinds me stressfully. There is only myself right now and these ideas bounce themselves off of walls and the holes in my head.

I never look at photographs and see just a day captured. There is never just face value in love and times that it was found or rediscovered. When we take our hands and reach out for days long dead, it is not merely flesh we wish to grasp, it's a feeling in the throat. It's an idea or time in which the fear of everything else is replaced with warmth without the bloodshed. The above line reminds me of a dream I had. Only two photographic moments remain with me. The first, I am running through a red light. I have no idea why, but I feel a high level of anxiety; my destination is vital. The camera on top of the stoplight flashes and catches me in the act of flight, but I don't care. The second moment, I am lying on a red carpet; it is the same color of the rug I had in my room as a child.

I feel a great sense of loss that I have felt very few times in my life. This feeling alone shocks me into waking up, I know there were many moments in between that shaped the fabric of this dream. I can't decide what happened. All I know is this feeling from the dream is one I have felt so seldom in my lifetime, more than any monsters clung to that red carpet of mine as a child, under fear and my bunk bed. I hope this isn't a premonition for the future, or I may just quit now.

Fingertips hit the keys at speeds I rarely hear. It is as if my mind is trying to outrun the idea that I am self-destructing to the point of complete loss. When the demons in your head vanish and you grow out of childish fears, you are left to your own destruction. There is not a single human being on this planet that can ruin you as well as yourself. I fear that I clutch the detonator while strapping the bomb across my chest.

Sub-conscious or not, premonition or random, I am afraid of where I have lead myself and the scent of gunpowder that stings from just far enough away to drive me insane.

X.

I could have sworn I was done writing for the night, like a ghost came into my head and stole my thoughts like a silent visitor trying to release me from myself. However, I'm doing dishes and scrubbing dirt from the bottom of my own gluttony. My hands get shriveled like the eight-year-old me just had a deep-sea scuba diving mission in the bathtub. I rub my hands together and create a sound that sends chills up and down my spine, like Father Time came and screamed all my mistakes down my throat and tried fishing for regret.

But the fish ain't biting. The lake has been dried up for far too long, and I'm left with soap running down the front of my shirt, with nothing more than a long fallen memory. A memory that somehow fell off the cliff of my mind into a 20-something-year abyss. It passes the awkward moments, like middle-school "loved" left unappreciated. It slides past the days I can't recall from when I was a small child, and before it falls away forever, it clings to one last gripe in my heart that was somehow left selfless.

The part of me that didn't allow me to be absorbed in the echo of my own mindless banter…

And so it climbed. It did not fall victim to a firefight between the ideals I held and the ones I know hold higher than gods, or devils, or whatever we should call them. This thought excited before pubescent insecurity suffocated every aspect of who I should have been, with the illusion of what a 14-year-old me wanted people to think, under the barbed wire that was memories of misspent anger towards the few people foolish and loving enough to pick up the pieces, even if they cut back and bleed your love unconditionally.

This memory brushed off all the dirt and unconditionally loved every misspent emotion. It cast no judgment because it was brought up in an era before I learned to hate, right before I took the advice of others like they mattered, treated opinions of insecurity like the gospel and left me a homeless prophet of a day we could never see. It moved past all of these things, and it found me in the familiar sound of rough hands rubbing themselves together.

I am an eight-year-old boy in a hospital chapel. I sit in a beautiful room alone. My legs are still short enough to not have to deal with the pressure of having them hit the floor. I dangle and wonder what all these symbols mean. My youngest brother is in another surgery for a syndrome he never asked for, one that will never give him back a life that he could have lived. No separation of fingers. Toes dangling from his own feet will change every perplexed look he will never be able to understand. Neither he nor I could have possibly understood the recovery ahead, the roadblocks, the setbacks, and the acts of naturalism I could have or would have asked for.

I try and take the mind of a small child and understand the complex of God and the innocent-but-self-centered thinking of an eight-year old boy, wondering why it's his brother that must hang from the noose of social comfort. Not that I thought of it in that way, or that I could have even known that years later, this would be a moment that struck me like my memory bank got robbed of all selfishness, that its only trails left behind were coins telling loathing stories of middle class woe. It pains me to look at my life in such a direct manner, and I would never wish to follow the trail, in fear it will show me too much honesty and I will not be able to find that eight-year-old boy again…the one that didn't care about anything but the safety of his brothers, a guardian with no training who couldn't even manage to hit better than seventh in the line-up of little league.

Yet somehow, this was me at my most beautiful, at my most fearful. Innocently I wondered if there was a man with a great beard and a grand big book, with my name alongside my brothers. After this stop in the micro-universe, we could possibly find something a little bit better, with one another and for all the best of each other.

I look at myself then and now. I would have felt shame at how many steps back I took in my own morality, if I wasn't so engulfed in who I still have the chance of being. When home is where the heart finds itself, X marks the spot, and here lies the best part of me, the part that knew all about you.

Y.

This one haunts me, with anti-climactic delusions of grandeur. I am wandering along with the idea that there is nothing. My questions frighten me, but the lack of answers horrifies me. This is the type of fear that turns hair white and peels paint off neglected homes on roads with rusted-over train tracks and untamed grass. In the fields of faith, I am with no altar. I burned all this wood for heat, and still I am freezing with doubt.

Splinters gouged out the savior's eyes, and now we just blindly grab for words with meaning. Still left with so little, feet slam against pavement like lovers that can't quite decide if lust can outlast hatred, or if it's one more thing to lose faith in. Language torments the mentally ill, hope promises recovery, and mankind rips it away. It is like the floorboards of neglected homes and their ill-kept terrain; the arguments still echo, but the lust buried itself in memories for no one to remember. It is like the blind, grabbing for an altar, coming up with ash and falling back with the sinking feeling of complete loneliness....

....Yet when I talk like this, it feels as if I have thrown together a puzzle with misshaped pieces that should form the word "lost" but they just can't fit together. The edges are jagged and stubbornly refuse to connect together with their own brothers and sisters. It should be a cry for help, but it is only so silent a sound that I can no longer remember if it even made a sound, or that was my own self-deprecation playing tricks on me. I am terrified of looking the fool, so I yell the loudest while I am alone, as if this brings me some great sense of joy that no one else could give me or hope to understand. I don't know what I am looking for, I only know that it is not the loneliness that I constantly praise. Whatever devil of the self rises up from me and enjoys seeing the pain of those who only wish to help me drowned in answers I refuse to acknowledge.

I am sorry to all those that came and went, the few who stayed, and the ones I can't quite remember. I remember our times together, and for the most part, I feel as if a most bitter meal crawled into the cavern of my stomach and called it home. I have a pension for guilt and a responsibility for the failing of friendships. It blinds me into thinking I am responsible for all these shortcomings I have come across in these past few years. I think of friends and call them neglected homes. I think of love lost and connect it with the sound of my heavy feet hitting the road beneath.

I think of my own insecurity and compare it to the idea of faith. The sound of fire hitting an altar or some other religious object is really the silence right before sleep, the last absent thought before I am taken away, only to wake up to more of the same but in a different day. It is one that brings me hope anew, but simmering at the edges of this hope is the knowledge that I had wasted the day before on so little. I am now with so few people, and those I have lost keep piling up, just like these words I write, searching for answers, coming up empty.

Without your friendship, there is merely just one more question that took your place. Where you once stood with me is now replaced with doubt. Both these events were self-induced. Forgive me for the word vomit and useless metaphors. I miss you, all while I question myself, maybe in another life, the only thought that rings with clarity through troubled thoughts.

Z.

Growing older means getting to watch everything you tried to love turn parasitic. I used to look at the features of love and thought of them as eternal ideas I could hold on to, while wearing a mortal's watch. My gears eventually stop turning in an endless clock, as they go on without me. You can't hang on forever and the grip loosens everyday, yet I like to pretend maybe I could fall forever once the last evidence of my fingerprints falls off this ledge, this life, this figment of no one's imagination.

I went from a hero to a hermit all the way to a maggot crawling in and out the nose of who I used to be. I'm worried I have stumbled onto the sad truth that we either lose everything we love and remember it dearly and motivationally so, or it lives with us long enough to show us its cracks and maybe we're too fractured to live with it. I safely watch from a distance as all the memories I had lose their purpose and motivation. I am so close to the end of these words right now, and still I do not feel closure. In fact, the door's wide open and the rain's crashing in, while the wind is whipping me around with its reminiscent hands, squeezing all the innocence out.

Maybe the world isn't dying. Maybe the Earth isn't falling. But its tenants are evicting themselves. This zero wraps itself around my throat and pulls me every which way but to all of you. I won't be another bitter note you sing, even if it leads me toward martyrdom. Nor is this another notch on a belt of regret. I didn't forget the things that brought us all, which is one reason I am alone.

Martyrdom is easy when you're trying to hide what lies under a shell of misaimed "fuck yous" and a plethora of loud yells that couldn't penetrate the truth if they were right in front of its face. Being alone means never having to come to terms with anything. Maybe that's what this is about and maybe there is closure, just not the type I saw coming around the bend. It's the kind that fell off a cliff and somehow burst into the flames of you before it could hit the ground. I saw every inch, felt every moment as if it played out in an eternity, or at the least my entire life. This is not true though, it was a few moments with an aftermath that still burns at my core.

I found closure, only after I lost everything I had. When the old cliché rings out like a church bell leading the lams home, "Trust no one," it should come with fine print, "especially not what you think you may want." But I was to blind to notice either way. Home is zero, wrapped around my throat. So far away from what this should have meant. I opened up a dictionary, to get a better understanding of "closure" and I didn't even make it. I drowned in your letters. The words filled my lungs like water, and that was all there was.

Goodnight.

Acceptance

1. "The Love We Leave"

I wipe the beads of sweat from my forehead
They're like a foreign intruder trying to break into my eyes
Sent by their leader, dry summer heat
I don't know what either of them want
But I'm waiting for them to break
It's 11pm now, and the sun has fallen back on the front lines of my porch
But the heat still stays
Indoors or out, it follows me
And I'm lying on the floor with the camouflage of a less lonely day
In hopes the heat will just drift above me,
That it will think sad days don't live here anymore
But even here, it follows me
I'm waiting for the cooling feel of comfort
And my clock slowly grinds itself to 2am
I can't ease myself from this
The heat has infiltrated my comfort
Turned my own blanket against me
And we're sweating out this war on a pillow turned battlefield

I'm counting casualties on the stripes of my sheets
I keep hopeful but my devil of doubt spits the most pessimistic warmth to kiss my ear
My clock painfully creaks…it's 2:01
I fear he's turned on me now, another enemy
I'm waiting on another minute
3am
4am
5
The same story told threefold, all waiting on the same ending
In the dead of night, your nemesis couldn't tame you
And soon you'll pick up speed
Soon you'll call for back up and all of this will be turned up
My windows will be overwhelmed and your general will shine through
Not even these shades will control you
You'll fight through
You'll force me out of this bed and right through the door
And instead of rising to face you, I'm plotting to fight you
If I know what's coming, how come I've yet to figure out how to beat you?

This question will pass the time 'til we meet again,
Maybe then my eyes won't be fixated on all I used to know
Regardless, here I am…

I used to know this life
Her eyes, the sky
Bright, but at times, clouds form around and a storm rages
The edges of its smile was the sun and my memory of her was the heat
What is this war really about?
Cause much like this summer, it keeps me from sleep
Both wars started when I wrote for the first time, "This life I used to know"
Both wars are fought on the edge of my mind
Both wars try and use my body against me and my bed
And my clocks wave the white flag and surrender
Now it's 7am, and all the love we leave
And I'm laying on the frontlines of this statement
Constantly reminded on what I used to have and all I used to know
An even though I'm moving on and fighting forward
I'm still being bitten at by the faults of forgotten days.

Protagonist:
The story starts out with our character in an evening of loathing, broken from
those who have betrayed and left him and isolating himself from those who
would never leave him. He beats himself mentally throughout an entire night.
He lets insomnia begin to rot his mental stability and ability to do what's right
for him. He completely pleases a world of naysayers and viciously penetrating
eyes by allowing his "devil of doubt" to "spit the most pessimistic warmth to
kiss his ear." It represents warmth because giving up is just so easy at this point.
It appears to be the only option, as he counts the casualties on the lines of his
sheets, stares into the nothing of dark, and wastes another night on things that
could care less about him.

2. Despair I Wrote

As these eyes flood me
Severed wings float with me
So walk on
These severed wings stay with me
Like hollowed hearts follow me
Oh, dear mistress, how I learn and loathe that one minute too late
Temptation wants this flood to kill my lungs with death's passing glance
Fair mistress called out again
Merely a whisper down the long hall of regret
Swallow the bitterness as she swallowed the regret I spoke

(Chorus):
Time....
Carry me where wings
Show me pictures of her face
And now stand still in this forever place
Where memories made this gold
Only to drop me in a life untold

Claws...planted in the shoulder
Taken to hell below and heaven above
Now release me
Fall again for thee
Memories that taunt with forked tongues that haunt
Ripped and ravaged from all I've ever done
Now with this life shunned, I'm sorry
This mistress shall never ponder these words again
And all I want is all I don't deserve
For all I have is all she gave to me
Take it away
Now
Forever

(Chorus)

She falls onto snow banks
Still I was told to give thanks
This forever winter awaits you

Look at what you had
Who you were
Let the cold remind her
It's a harsh reminder
And as tomorrow fills reborn lungs
Now fall into your eyes third heart
Live your life
Pay.
Her.
Price.
Mistress no longer carries you with bitter claws
So now we thaw
Fall into my heart by ripping my chest apart
Now foreign.
Forever winter.
Walk on.

(Chorus)

Maybe death is a gift
Life is the price we pay
If I take today away I rip the pain away
When will I learn
The answer in death I yearn
Living life is how you earn

Antagonist:
Even though this song appears after "The Love We Leave" on the record, the chronology of these songs are the same; they occur at the exact same time. Remember the "pessimistic warmth" he was hearing? Well, this song is it. His devil, his insecurities are telling him that everything he has lost in his lifetime and all the misfortune he has found was his own fault. He's supposedly "ripped and ravaged by all he's ever done" when these actions of negativity have been brought upon him, not caused by him. Once all of his insecurities have weakened him, they tell him, "Maybe death is a gift." This alarms our character into finally waking up. So ironically, just when his demons feel they have their collective claws "planted in his shoulder," it actually turns out that this gives him hope. His lowest moment is also his epiphany.

3. Seasons Change

Dear Jane,

    I am writing to you today because I can't seem to remember all your features that made last year's bloom so full of life, so full of hope and potential.

    I filed a missing persons case on you, but slowly it is being lost under piles of cases far too similar to this. There is a police sketch of you, hanging on the corner of my mind, but the edges are burned off from all the candles of your casual goodbyes, and the artist was blind. And so I walk along the razors edge of my tongue, handing out flyers that plead on page, "Have you seen these memories?" And in this newfound world I live in, of the mute and the colorblind, bitter lips mouth the words "no" and walk on, leaving me under the trees that seemingly know that you're gone. Because all they do is fall from the sky you once opened up and crumble at my feet

    So, if you read this today, tomorrow, or some day after I'm gone, just know there was once a time where I took this pen and I tattooed your name in this letter, in hopes you'd come home. So now I stick it in this bottle and I send it out to you.

Sincerely,
John Doe

I just wanna fit all the right parts on one page
All the right words in one letter
And I wanna send it back in time,
To the perfect day, at just the right time
Where I search for the perfect words
All these days I do is lay in change
I was bound to your ground
And I was tied to the smell of Autumn's breath
Laying on the lips of limbs and leaves
As these trees dropped them on me
Even though Fall trees tell me there is so much color
I have never felt so gray
And underneath these lies, all I see are branches longing for life
Clinging to the day of rebirth
The night grows long, and the days and I are short of time

Like your eyes on my mind and your hold on my thoughts
And now, as this snow drops, and this ground is freezing
And I am frozen, but I am burning

(Chorus):
This pen is my brush and I wrote a picture for you
It screams all the subtle things of you
Blind hands feel for Summer days
But in seasons change....
This pen is my brush and I wrote a picture for you
It screams all the subtle things in you
Blind hands feel for Summer days
But in seasons change
They hold on to what winter portrays

And I've surrounded myself in this frozen hellhole
Where I can't bother to feel warm or cold
Where the air matters not
Because I can't even feel a thing
Is it me that has become so calloused and unforgiving?
From the countless hours I spent watching you walk away from windows that
I sat
The despair I wrote has become the sorrow I sing
And I'm so tired of bending over backwards
For just one glance of a season long passed
But I can't help but want to take in the taste and smell of those cool night airs
In which I held your smile higher up than the sky
God forgive me for taking five steps back
But I miss the footsteps
And I want to walk them,
Even if it's for one last time
Though they're washed away
And long forgotten by everyone but me

(Chorus)

I want the day to come down
I want the rain to come down
I want to feel the changing of these days back to life under my fingertips
As the ground I grip under pain's palm

As they write patterns of yesterday
Traced with the thoughts of today and the hope for tomorrow
I want to hear the trees give birth to the beauty that winter aborted
Feel my feet walking under a warm wind
Carrying words that I thought I left behind
For one moment, I wanna feel the way I did back then
So I can capture it all in my lungs and exhale
So I can remember what it was like to lay content in all the smaller parts of
you
With my eyes closed shut and my arms holding tight
Under pen pushing paper with ink bleedings words
This is the letter I have written
But when I have awoken, I have found that I am still unbroken

Protagonist:
After the nightmare that was the first two parts of this record for our character, all spun in one evening, this person realizes that it's time to choose between the life he's been given and the life he wants. However, still being naive, he writes a letter to his past life "in hopes it would come home," yet as he sends it, he feels as if he's "sending it off to sea" in the sense that he knows it will not change anything, it's a lost cause, and it will not find the person by whom he wants it to be read. This leads him into memories and nostalgia. He WANTS to feel old memories; the weather reminds him of certain times, and he wants to change the way the wind blows so that he may be able to close his eyes and take himself back. He's finally mourning and purging all of these things by verbalizing them. By admitting that he misses his old life, he feels he can hopefully let go of it. He admits that he is "blindly" searching for something, leading him to be ready to admit that he's "tired of bending over backwards for just one glance of a season long passed." He begins to accept so much of how he feels and realizes that writing the letter did nothing, but coming to the understanding that leading to his old life will bring him nothing allows him to being overcoming that. This "coming to terms" can be found in the third verse. Now, in this song I used the phrases "I want" or "I wanna" over and over, almost to the point of being repetitive. The reason for this is that I wanted this song to center around the self. In fact, the original version didn't have half the amount of this phrasing, but after writing the majority of the album, I went back and re-wrote some of the lyrics because I focused so much on how I reacted to certain things and I wanted this song to be a turning point from "This is how it makes me feel" to, "This is how I want it to make me feel."

4. Old Home

How many more times will faded portraits guilt me into waking in a bed of regret
In a "home" long abandoned,
And the only taxes paid on this property,
Are that of another day I should have left?
I never miss a payment.

I trace over footsteps walked long ago
I plead to broken staircases for them to find a way to light this old home
For you've blackened my sun and cheapened the moon
It ran me dry of ink, watching you burn pages not yet touched
So I crawl through memories of a house warmed by this blanket of dust
And I'm looking for a way to write these letters to you
The seasons have changed, but I'm still writing letters to Jane and signing them Doe
I'm still trying to look at fall trees through the eyes of the colorblind
But all I do is trace eyes over ghosts that don't even bother to haunt this old home

Yet this old house has numbed me to new days
And I've lost the thirst for better ends
How many more times will I watch this clock tick over the same hour?
How many more bars will be timed by the tock of the same minute?
How long will I watch the grandfather golden of days gone by
Rust in a casket of today?
I should send you off to sea, I swear I know
But I fear the loneliness without that familiar sound

I've blacklisted my own number
But regardless, I've already cut the chord
Like a newborn into this world, I've separated myself
From those who've helped bring me here
I've gone from a victim to a martyr
In the amount of time it takes to count our misfortunes
And idling for so long has led my own mistakes to bleed out
All over the hinges of these doors
Attempting to rust shut
To close me out of a room that would lead me through the same repetition

And from what I'm told, that's the definition of hell
And that is fine with me
So allow me to sit next to Judas
Because I've done such a wonderful job of betraying myself

At this point, stick an apple in my mouth
And roast me under the fire of a life unlived
Now it's time to feed my demons

How many more nails until I've finally closed myself off?
Until this house becomes a coffin
When the soil of my sins crashes down in waves and buries these windows?
Losing all view of what I have already lost touch with
Until the days past, has run out of air for my lungs to grab onto

Anything can become comforting if met with enough time
Even the bitter taste of disappointment
Allow me to wash it away with content
Let my feet callous over as I walk on broken images and glass of days I fell short
Which only makes the healing of these wounds in days content that much
sweeter
As I lay here sinking, not swimming
Thinking and not writing
Wasting until I die, rather than living
I know now that my wants and my needs have submerged themselves in
happier days
And these aches in my chest are really only my happiness calling from paradise
Awaiting my return

These feelings wonder of the day in which
This smile will not be washed away by the lingering grasp of discontent
Where I will not have to fear sleep because the thought of waking to another
twenty-four
Will bring peace and not pain
To find this new start
So I may feel the weight of the ocean upon my back
As it puts out the fire of yesterday's wants
Leave me with the wet and decaying ashes of today (as a memoir of my
efforts)
As I arise in flight from them tomorrow

(Outro)

Don't allow me to live another moment mourning what has only once held me back

I need not the wisdom to find what better awaits me on dry land someday

But rather the strength to fight against this current alone

For what has kept me afloat in breaths past

Now clings to my ankles and lowers me down

I've let your words blacken my sun and cheapen the moon

So I've chosen not to write by day or night

You've run me dry of ink

Because you burnt your pages and prose

So I'll chisel words onto walls

They bleed

Needing not the night or the day

I will burn my thoughts so deep into the foundation of this home

That it will scream in splinters and peeling words

I will tear the brightest blue out of the sky an write it on your reflection

To force you to face yourself, to see my words

To make you see the lines in your face

To view the brightness of the day

I'll burn every blanket I once used to cover my eyes

Send a smoke signal S.O.S. to a new chapter

Please, I need to breath in the hope of that new day

To breathe out the day for old ends

And when the smoke and embers can't reach high enough to kiss my utopia

In search of bliss

I will light this old house ablaze

Every word I wrote

Every creek in wooden steps I've walked

I light fire to every lonely day, violent night and silent rising of the sun

I hope this is enough to reach you,

For I am burning all I have ever had to send you this

May every lesson darken your lungs

I hope it coughs out a better day

I hope the smoke of every fallen dream and desperation mistake blinds your eyes

Cause you don't deserve to watch me start anew

Antagonist/Protagonist
Of course, the negative side of our character cannot allow this newfound understanding to burn out the flame of pessimism as it has no place for fear, and he will soon learn that's all that his negativity is -- fear of not being quite good enough.

(verse 1-2, antagonist)
He "blacklists" his own number, isolates himself from loved ones, and keeps himself in an abandoned home, which acts as a bomb shelter against finding better days. The negativity he finds realizes, "I should send you off to sea, I swear I know/but I fear the loneliness without the familiar sound." He's fallen so far down the rabbit hole of isolation that he even admits it. He's comfortable in repetition, in hell.

(verse 3 – outro, protagonist)

Realizing that all of his pain is really just his happiness calling from paradise as a way of motivation, he comes to a realization that everything he feels, he's bringing upon himself. He has LET the people in his life blacken his sun and cheapen the moon, and he used these reasons as an excuse not to write. His reactions to others' actions were completely on him; only he's responsible. He becomes more intuitive and realizes he doesn't need the light of another to have enough sight to write everything he needs to say. He burns down the old home, old memories and old seasons. He uses it as a way to call out to better days hoping they will see.

This song and "Seasons Change" go hand in hand, the former being about longing and the latter about the isolation and the inability to give lifeless items up. The clock, the blanket of dust, and even the home itself all represent the things in life we love and have lost yet can't move on from. This song is rooted in my issue of giving up meaningless items because of the memories I hold with them. In the end, this song is about struggle and ultimately overcoming and burning down all that holds negative memories that don't teach us anything. Sometimes, the only lesson in pain is walking away from it.

5. Time to Let Go

I'll never forget you…
You saw me at my worst, and you related
My faults brought you comfort and the loneliness
Of the cross you used to bear by yourself
And quicker than that glance
We doubled our burdens as one
And lifted the weight of our minds off our beaten blow
Quicker than us, the collective you and I
But in a moment, a second glance...
Time caught up and tied our sins to our limbs
And watched as we pulled each other apart
I stitched myself back to life only to look at the scars unbroken mirrors
The outline of your fist still screams at me

And I move on
Slower than my pain
But not quick enough to catch another glance
I find these stiches harder to find everyday
They're no longer a road map back to you
Everything has moved on
Nothing stays. Moving on.
No blood to beckon when it seeped through the cracks in facades long ago

I find myself on this night tracing over time passed again
I wonder why I miss the intimacy of your insecurities
Hitting my faults with the beauty they created
I'm on the eve of change
But snakes still wrap around your fruit and whisper words I used to pen
For this, I still doubt
Every breath, every word, every step, and all these things in between
It's my fear, it hates when I progress
It wants me to cage in my rage
And count the distain in these eyes
So in the 11th hour of change, I want to sink back to a ship full of holes
Taking water in a sea full of loathing
I'll come back and we'll drown together

In all of our wrongs we were too afraid to right
You made me feel Heaven in all of my Hell
And we changed nothing
No wars fought in our name
No battle worth the struggle
So now your face barely resumes anything human
Still, I want to bury my face in the neck of lost days
For the remainder of my own
Close my eyes so tight they forget how to see

You're walking hand in hand with a world that promises you wings
But you're getting closer and closer to the edge
And there's a sea at the edge of that cliff and the waves below are writing your eulogy
In Old English font with every powerful crush against those jagged rocks
So when you fall I want you to think of me
I warned you,
"Words without action while chasing dreams is
A lighter with no fluid trying to spark a flame."
And now you're just drowning in all that blue
I know you're not spending your last seconds
Crashing against reality, wondering about me
But I'm going to tell you anyway…

I'm on the gray side of town
The view's nothing special and it gets a little worse every day
At least it's dry, though.
I used to wish for the water drowning your lungs
And the old me from a life that seems so far wishes I could join you
In the depth of who I am I still do
From the lowest of the low which fell through the lowest level of hell
In my own personal canto
But now I see you're sinking alone
While I'm sailing in nothing
Safety is a prophet whose tablet was cracked and I can't see his scripture
Just call me a born-again Realist with a taste for the bitter things in life
Those words won't save you now
Those syllables won't save you from the sea

(Protagonist/Antagonist)

Realizing he's gone past the point of no return and left his old life behind has also allowed him to realize that his happiness and his sadness must co-exist. Neither can fully take over this man because he needs both. He now comprehends that they help him grow, they make him a better human being by accepting that the world will bring him down, and that there are beautiful lessons in scars. He returns to the sea where he sent out his previous letter (the intro of Seasons Change), only to find everything he used to love drowning. His instincts are to help and save, as they've always been, but the merging of these two heavy emotions in him have taught him that there are some things and some people you can't save. So he goes up to the drowning lives and he gives them a new letter. The words of this song are this letter, and then he lets them go. Sometimes letting go is the hardest thing to do, and in those situations, they tend to be the only thing.

6. Portrait

I don't want to be numb
I don't want to self-medicate with the shallowest of lows
I don't care how far down the rabbit hole I fall
I don't want to lose the sharp hint of pain at every mistake I see around me
This hurt is who I am, and it may be all I have right now
So I'll hold it close, like a favorite memory or a childhood dream
This is how I feel
And this is who I am
I'd ask you the same, but I fear you can't even hear me ask this question
Strength isn't something we're given
It's something we find
And how foolishly we forget that it lies in our eyes
Every second it beats inside of us all
So why are we so afraid to feel?
Let the blood pump throughout my veins
And let every time it escapes my skin, let me feel it
This is your body's way of screaming out to you,
"Even if we bleed, and even if we fear every step may be our last,
This is how I let you know we're still alive."

'Cause the sad truth of every unwritten book
Every picture frame that should hold a point in time
But now only rusts
Every canvas left untouched
Every song left unsung
And every closed mind left ignorant
Is that idle ways forge forgetful days
And how quickly these days blend
Like a clock master with broken ties to father time
We're wasting minutes-turned-to-hours
And these weeks have turned to months
How we'll one day rock in our chairs
Drowning in a sea of "what ifs"
I know in old age you'll be tired of swimming
You're drowning for nothing
Breath in
Feel the wind
Feel the fire

Feel the jaws of the hell hounds biting at your heals
Goddamn it
My love
My enemy
My brothers
My sisters
Just feel something
I plead with every calendar-marked day you're about to live
Feel the tears you need to cry
Feel them to release these demons
Right now

Living life is not determined by the air you take in
It's marked by what you do with it
The words we speak in between these breaths
The lives we touch, the life we share
There is sweat begging to be released from your pours
Sweat out every disgusted look you've been given from eyes that wish they
could fill Your shoes
Come outside, rain or shine
Feel your life

(Acceptance/Voice of Reason)
Remember that "faded portrait" in "Old Home?" Well, our character in the
final track begins a new one in a new life, using the brightest colors he shares
with us in hopes of helping others. It leads him to the conclusion that "idle ways
forge forgetful days." He vows that while he knows he will feel pain, he will take
every time he sheds blood as a lesson waiting to be learned. The portrait tells of
shedding fears and not allowing one to hold their own potential back. This is a
plea to a world that gives up everyday, that you must accept the fact that we live
in a world full of people that don't care, realize it, and move on. Don't let any
mistake or loss of any type of love stop you. Life is a gift.

"Portrait" was an interesting song for Pat and I to work on, simply because it
took forever to figure out on my end. Pat had a rough idea of what he wanted to
do with it sometime in late 2010. The version on the album is almost a complete
overhaul, but the concept was still in place. However, I went through about
three different versions of the song before we settled on "Portrait" in April 2011.
When I was living at Drew University in December 2010, I wrote "The Day
After." After that fell flat, I wrote "Mountains We Climbed" that summer before I

settled upon the album version the following spring. For better or worse, though, these poems were written during important times of my life and were supposed to be a part of the album, so I have included "The Day After" and "Mountains We Climbed" in this book.

"The Day After"

I find my face holding up sweat that weighs me down
From the overwhelming thoughts of my hours slowly creeping by
They weigh down the soles of my feet like concrete under a portrait sea
Drowning my hours away
Lowering me down
As I seemingly run through my thoughts
The jaws of my passing life bites down and drains my blood
May this bring frost to your lips
For the cold thoughts run through me
May this blood burn your thoughts
From the boiling point my veins have reached
More importantly…
May this blood give you purpose
May it give you reason
For the amount I have seen
And the amount I have shed
Can only be conjured by the blood you can't drain
The supply kept behind bloodshot eyes
The blood that drips
When we bare our teeth at enemies
And at my past days
That shred calendars and coagulated hours
That gel together in misery
And may my blood poison the weak
Because
My strength defies reason
My strength relies on tomorrow
My strength defines prevailing

As I fall across these days' end
As broken promises
And bruised knees
Beat the day light out

And as this sun
Swings from one side to the other (and another)
I walk off this life limping
And just as I feel that my effort and my success

Are separated by so many miles
I am given an open letter from the sky
Delivered by the coming night
And this sunset reassures my push forward
Of inches turned to yards

And in another ten or so....
I will be filled with a new day
So I respond to this letter with aching lungs
With my own sweat, tears, and ink
Of fighting through this night
This doubt
This loneliness
Even at the darkest point
When my eyes can't count the miles
(passed)
And my eyes can't see the pavement
(passed)
I shine on
And even when the line blurs
Between miles passed
And the miles left to go
I walk on, the sunrise warming my back
Walk on
Shine on
Live on

No more doubt
No bitter words freezing my mouth
No hesitation numbing my mind
This is the morning after
This is survival and this is rescue
This is all I should have known
Not before but after I fall

"Mountains We Climbed"

These are the days
In which I can hardly lift my lids to my brow
When the gaze in the mirror breaks from the stress on my eyes
This decision to live
This acceptance of life
Comes with a high price I pay in sleep
And God only knows the amount of debt my eyes owe this pillow
Because I haven't slipped easily under the covers of my reflection for so long
I toss and turn at the thought of ease
And this mess of tangled insomniacs' sheets is where I seem to stay
This is faith
This is the fool
I know the need of both because they are me in my happiest of dreams
If I am to die a fool's death, knee deep in my own tangled nerves
Weaving "what if" and "what could have been" alongside my eyes
Then I'll live the life of the faithful
A life lived of running across bridges that may exist
Only under the feet of my hope and the passion for getting across this mountain

So even if this bridge gives out and my hope dims to such a low light
That this day collapses under my stress
Well then, the refreshing water of reality will hit the back of my neck
With things I can't control
At least it allows me to dry off in your sun
Which allows me just close enough to flicker but not catch fire
It gives me the strength deep down
To set myself ablaze
And in those moments
I will use your glow to read out my future on this burning palm
No matter how much this burns, it will not turn my hope to ashes
It will never engulf my faith
I will use it to read the rest of my life
Regardless of broken covers and burnt edges on these pages
Each one will be filled
Each one will tell of this
Even the most crumpled and crippled page of them all
Where all ink should be faded and illegible
Where none of these words should shine to you

And that page will tattoo the brightest words on this page
That page is called Today
And until my time has come,
I won't allow its last words to read as:
"The End"

Every day, I question if these healing wounds are reminders of how far I've
come
Or signs that this world is that much closer to breaking me down.
For the wind may cool the back of the neck and push me forward
But the sun shines down and burns my eyes
Trying to keep me from seeing every lesson within the battle and the burning
heat.
Which will win?
What brings me further... or burns me back?
My feet feel the fire, as it seems that they tread slower and slower
This gravel grinds beneath the ball of the foot
I wonder where am I going and how far have I truly come
If I need to ask the question, I see that I am yet to deserve the answer
Every second of pain is a sign that we're alive
It holds a lesson on how to better the next
So where does that leave me right now?
As this chapter closes and the ink dries on all the previous pages
What have I learned?
That I believe in everyone
Yet right now, most importantly, I believe in you
And I believe in me
And I believe that this is our final push
I believe that we haven't beaten our demons yet
But I know each and every blow may be the last
That final shot we take may just break down everything we've been afraid of
And everyday congratulate yourself on the day you've fought through
I can't tell you which of us will be blessed to see another sunrise
Or even what will happen from here on out
But you never know, so never stop trying
Never give in to the forked tongues of your doubts
Don't give thoughts to the ghosts that live in memories
When the only thing you taste on your own tongue is bitter
Cause one day the life we've feared
Will become the mountains we've climbed.

From Nothing Comes
Nothing
(Living on Dead Ends)

1. "Here Again"

Here I am again
Searching deserted streets
Looking for an answer of sorts
For a question we all ask
Sung by so many
But the sun fades and the search must wait
It goes on
Forever, until even that is gone
Not that this was ever eternal
Yet I am so tired of passing the same signs
During a certain time that keeps telling me the same thing
Welcome back
And goodbye
Rinse and repeat on my childhood street
So the sun sets again
With a gasoline scent
And so I wonder, if tonight's the night
It all goes up, only to go out
A moment's glow
With an endless silence
Just give me that
Even though I know
I'll just make my bed in the aftermath
Lay my head to sleep in the rubble
Instead of moving on to new roads
With better-lit signs

"What a great day to be alive," said the dead man who didn't know it yet.

And so I've been told
The first through the wall
Will break the most bones
But broken hands breed empty pages
With a head full of doubt
So my fear repeats
When I'm asking for things I can only give myself
But I'll keep going on with an out-of-tune pitch
Simply because

One moment in time is enough
Anything more and I'm useless
When I lose myself
Is when I ask everyone to stay
After the fact
When I come to realize
That nobody leaves this life
Without losing (a part of) themselves
So I'm to the point
Where I'm just trying to save any part of me
When I'm running away
To the same old grave
This is not who I am
Nor what I was meant to be
Fading facades frighten me
When I start to see what I should have been
Where I should have started
Forever Ago
Not even that stays the same

I was never meant to be this way
This insecure
When I've never opened up
I should have known
It would lead to you pulling it apart
A final plea so desperate
When I finally start to feel the wall my back has always been against
Too busy preaching
Instead of confessing
Screaming out, "You're to blame"
To avoid my own
Maybe if I scream loud enough
The words in my head could die down
But it was never enough
So take it limb from limb
Throw away all of my dead ends that I've been living on
So maybe
Just maybe
Something better can grow from them
In time

With enough purity
Yes, well meaning kindness
The things we forget to give ourselves
We could give to each other
And we can move
We won't have to live here anymore
Even though we have so much more to admit

I felt it
Those cold hands dug into my shoulders
I knew it was you
I turned around and found
That there was absolutely nothing or no one that I knew
A crowded street with empty eyes is all I could find
The buildings I used to remember
And the times I would have recalled
Have been stripped

When denial debunks the reality you've set in your head
Two-dollar words made from 50-cent syllables
Can't cover your eyes and erase your memories
Nothing and nowhere
The corners we come from
The ride we'll wait for
The one that never comes
So in the meantime
I just want to sabotage everything
When everything I fight for is losing dignity
And everyone I love is so deafening, I can't even hear it
Like when we're going so fast
You would swear we weren't moving
And when the voice pierces me into nothing
All I can hear is the rain
And it reminds me
That we're still under the same sky
So when the water turns to fire
And it kisses our cheeks with a final performance
I'll take my last bow
And as you do yours
I hope the last thing you see

Is the roses I'll throw at you
The way they'll hit you
And the thoughts you'll have
I'll never know them
And I'll wonder
What it is that you wonder
When I find the end
When I hit that wall
And all I see will crumble
It swallows me whole
And takes me home
All that rubble
That I am becoming

2. "Hear Me Now"

So I'm looking for sanity
In all the words I never said
I won't be afraid of a world that won't love
Anything I've ever done
When I won't search for something
That I lost inside of me
Faithless am I
When I won't believe in myself
Or you
Just because
The eyes of many applaud the pen that breaks
And there's nothing else to write with
The need for only two dancing pupils
To watch me as I work
Lashes weave in and out
The blink of an eye
The blink of a moment
To refill the working mind
To see those lips move upward
Brighten my hunger
Give me a reason
That I search for in vain
Shine the sun of days in which I could recount every second
And blind the night that took it all away

I remember the lavish sky
Drifting away under the blanket of that July heat
I could remember every detail
The brightest of red and the darkest of orange
Filled my mind
In my darkest moment
I rely on moments like this
In my weakness
So I'd burn off the fingertips of all those concubines
Scar their touch forever
Let all others who fall trapped…in their flesh, that they've been tainted
All so I could feel your own tainted touch one more time
The tip of the finger

The edge of the print
The knuckle
And the nails
I'd cut off the tongues of all the negative words of my past
That scream promises never kept
And all the negative words people will speak
Only after I rip the taste buds from severed tongue-in-cheek quotes
Just to taste another day
Any day
Anywhere

Even after all of this…
When I question the insomniac that rants in my ears
In the darkest of nights
When I search for the child that peacefully finds rest
In the most thriving of storms
I'd sever the nose off this lifetime
Forget the smell of defeat
In fact, I'd sever all senses
To find a worthwhile ending
But until then
This is all you'll read
These final words will find no peace in your eyes or mine
Purgatory of words
A soul that never loved or hated
Senseless as this has all become

3. "I Didn't Realize"

I didn't even realize it was Autumn
Until my eyes played connect the dots with the leaves
The ones left behind
I put them together with an outline of every foul word I said
Every passing word screamed guided me
Oh, misguided me
I felt the cold gravel to be paved under me
And I knew it weathered the worst of days
An so it would after I was gone

Maybe it took the visual of shorter days and lifetimes alike
To realize that nothing stays
Nor do we truly want it to
Is this my greatest find or the most foolish shortcut I could take?
I'll know by how much regret pours from my skin
When I'm given the mistaken glory of burning away quickly
There's no phoenix and I feel I won't rise from anything

Forgive me
For something I haven't even done
How well we truly know each other
Yet how false it is that we wish to change
Because
We all long for something new
When summer is nothing like we remember
A prologue for bitter cold that heals nothing
No matter how we wanted it to, it's the bitter cycle

Just
Wishing for something
Grabbing for anything
We lose something in between
While we find even less
So by the end of our time, we're merely regret with aged skin
Cut out my eyes before I can see what I've become
Not like you
But my own definition of you
So before I have to see myself

As an ungrateful sack of bones
Waited to be buried under another day
One that won't be remembered nor where I was left

I didn't realize before it was too late
Even thought only time can truly tell me this
Or so I'm telling myself when I'm fishing for excuses
Because compliments aren't biting today
When I'm far too co-dependent
So now, it's half past the vultures circling above me
Closer with every line
And pessimistic syllable I spat
When I look above I think,
"I hope I can still bring some positivity to the self."
In fact, I know I have to
But if not, the joke's on them
They'll be nothing left
By the time they're close enough to get me
If I go on like this
With the same selfish decisions
The funeral pyre will have burned out by the time they fly down
There won't be much when they dig in
It's so much harder to write without the visions of others
The world's venom that stings my eyes was always just an excuse
One that I can now see, since it's been wiped away
The self-inflicted wound always heals the hardest
Serving as a reminder for all I've let pass by

So no, I didn't realize it was Autumn
That's only one of many beautiful times I have let pass me by
My fault
This time it's on me
Oh God, what have I done?

4. "Cold Corners"

The Gods we wish for won't answer
When...4
Faces change
Days disappear
Before night gives way to another
But I'll never forget the way the air stung my lungs
Like the cold paralyzed them
For the time they shared
I feel winter in my throat
At the hint of a name
The kind of cold that touches the bottom of my stomach
It sickens me
Especially when

I use to drive along
With no destination
Or understanding of time
Because of this
There will always be roads I'll avoid
Faces I'll never forgive
Even though they're forgotten
You can put yourself back together
But there are just some things you can't escape
Now they're a part of me
But they're all in my head
So when I choose to react to them
There's no blaming others
When you let them in
Wolves may rest at your front steps
But you don't have to invite them into your bed
Giving them rest when you find less
You know what makes devils dance
So stop singing their songs

We swear our naysayers dig our graves
But the dirt that makes home under our fingernails,
They tell me a different story
I could have sworn them clean

But that changes nothing
We mistake our wings for backbreaking burdens that we try to uplift
But they remind us of moments just out of reach
Blurred-out faces
With voices too quiet to here
But how they made me feel stay with me
So much time wasted on trying to remember
As I try recount every blade of grass and the exact
Measurements of the sun
I'm a trashcan baby looking for a cradle fire to soothe me
To take me in

Ghosts are real.
They live in my head
And they weed out these memories
So they have enough room to sleep in
To make their nest
I dug at my skull for days
Dried blood-caked fingernails tell of their trail
And I just can't get them out
But it's not their fault
They know what they do
They understand who they are
Yet I clearly do not
That's why I let them lay and find rest
While I'm wide awake
Words flood the page
But I'm the one who's drowning
Upstream
Downstream
Doesn't matter when you can't take the air in
What you do is not right
But at least you're confident
I can't recover when I don't know where I'm broken
Or even where I am
I'm walking
While
While they're waiting for their howls and screams to be met
With the voice that makes these ears bleed
Everyday they're let down

They know what they do
You know as well
Stop hiding
Wounded hands can heal
After they bleed out all the evidence I need to find
Just to realize
That I only fall short
When I'm to afraid to let myself be afraid
That I may fall short

5. "Burial"

1

There's just something about you
Every time I see your face, I grind my teeth to dust
Every time your name is mentioned
I flinch like the wind was knocked out of me
By the thought of all the ignorant things you do.
I'm sorry.

If my arms could grant me a two ton hammer
I'd swing it at your mouth
Let's see how hard you bite down on the apple of all your addictions now
I hope you can't break the skin
This isn't a game and this joke was never funny to me
But you'll find the easy way out
While I'm looking for the right way in
They're never the same
Unlike you
And I'm brought back to all the things you do
Every little self-absorbed error you make
All the enabling whisperers you seem to surround yourself with
"Just one more," they laugh
When there really is no hammer
And your razor teeth bite right down to the core
Of your addiction and my insecurity
And the only outlet is between the lines of this verse
Yet even that isn't enough
Not when I'm sorry that I'm really not that sorry

2

When I can't sleep
But can't be awake
Face the errors in my way
Find the strength to fight for me
So I dance between the four
A square with rigged edges

Attempted to be pushed
Through a circular peg

3

Can I face my ghosts and lock away the child I still seem to be?
It all just seems too much for me
When I'm wasting all my money down wishing wells
Praying for an answer
Begging for a solution
When I don't quite know the question
Only to fall right in it, finding every un-granted wish
Throw me down a shovel
Tell me to dig my own way out
I'll only use it to dig my own grave
I want it to be personal
Not a one-size-fits-all
Isn't this just like me?
Isn't it just like me to bury me?
When you just want me to dig through to the other side
Mountains and molehills are all the same
When you're blindly grabbing for stability
In soil soft enough to sink into your fingernails

4

So I'll just lash out childlike
I can't trust anybody
Who tries so hard
To force themselves into endless clichés
You won't find tomorrow at the bottom of the bottle
Or the end of a barrel

5

I'm sorry
I've left it all behind
Because I can't see me growing old with you
But I can't even see me growing old with me

The black clouds want to grab me up
And choke me on every rainfall tear
From a duo of bastards passed and angels fallen
But there's just nothing here anymore
And in all honesty,
The only thing that ever was, is now nothing that will ever be
I can't decide how the story will end
Too bad I forgot how it started
My path is too covered to see
With all this sin clinging to my feet
And all of these hands grab up from the walking stones
They dig me down
Soft soil and hardened hands
Dragging me down

6

I'm screaming to the sky
And I'm begging to the ground
But nothing from nowhere hears me
And I look down to see
At what's dragging me to the dirt
Suffocating on soil and all I see is me
A bitter, broken, beaten, sinful, sorry me

7

Yes, in the dark of a night I no longer see
The young man I was still looks familiar
But there have been so many sunrises since that time
And these are the thoughts I have in that one single moment
One that is over, done, and gone
I wish I could dig this pencil deep enough
To show you how much I loved you
But then it would just be jet-black nothing
It's the end that I fear

The criticism ruins my hunger
Detrimental to my sight

You scream words like "wanting" and "needing"
I know I'm not the definition for you
Close the book
Burn the pages
Until the remains can't keep you warm anymore
Even if it could
It wouldn't be enough
There's a cold I could never touch
Or one that I never thought could exist
I tried to burn through you
I just burnt myself out
And the only evidence this ever existed is my need to vomit
Kiss the tiles
Make love to the floor
Send all your dead ends out the mouth
That once compelled to speak of such promises
'Cause they all come back up
Chewed up and half-eaten lies
The smell will never leave my lips
It taints the smile
Stains the teeth
Cracks the skin
And breaks the smile lines
Or so I think as I look in the mirror
And beat myself with this book
Hoping to find the answer for you
The definition of a piss poor human being
But words just don't you (in)justice
Not a single one can understand

6. "Erase"

I erase every word I write these days

When I find so much fault in everything else
I seem to lose so much of myself

Shaking at the foundations of what I built
Is the voice of a world gone mad
Lost inside all of its excess
But it's breaking me down
Leaving me vulnerable to all I see around me
Even when I try to filter it all through me
To make some sense
Of a world that cares for nothing
Past the inches in front of its face
And the hunger in its heart
When it doesn't build on the love of the few
It makes a home of the harlot for the many
And these moments of anxiety connect themselves closer and closer
When I'm sinking lower and lower
So If I'm up caught up to my neck in their words
And drowning in their judgment
When will I breathe free?
Where will I seek shelter?
How will I erode myself of the negativity
When even I can't build on the positive?

I practice what I preach
In a world that sees the good as blasphemy
And they're burning all my books
To warm their hate
So they may dry off their own irrational gaze
That they give to me and one another alike
Simply to spite
I've walked your path
I've seen your eyes
I know what they tell me
That I'm lost and they won't let me belong
When I'm homeless in heart

And morally weighing myself
On their scales
While self-conscious of my mortality
I'll seek approve outward
And end up beating myself inward
Yet it's obvious
When the many outweigh the few
The cries of better days get drowned out
In the laughter of oppression
You and I humor them when we speak up
Because they can't hear and they refuse to see
Senseless in the most evident of ways
For when your love is as pure as your outrage of everything you've ever seen
They'll cast you aside
Wonder where you went wrong
And you can reply,
"When I found your world, when I started losing me."
For when you seek success in their praise
You'll never rise up half as high as you should
But you'll be torn down twice as fast

So where does this leave all of me?
With a bunch of words
Compiled onto lines
That were saved from slaughter
Thoughts viewed as better than swine
But is it just the same old song?
The same plea, to a world that won't hear
Repetition is hell
You can find me in the inferno
While somehow still sinking in the sand
And drowning while buried from the neck below
So the flames really are eternal
But I'll keep burning
Screaming and preaching
Suggesting and proposing
In a world without humility
And an appetite for the excessive
I'll keep feeding it the regret I feel
To purge an endless pit

With the same old cry
A song and dance that had its curtain called
Swansong?
No, I'm starring down the barrel of a never-was song
With a trigger-happy mistress called temptation
And she is begging to blow my thoughts away into the sea
To be carried away and forgotten
Until it is more myth than anything
But if you find yourself in the sea of sorrow
Grab onto these thoughts
It's all we have
Until we need not scream these words
Until this isn't just foolish bursts of a pen
Until then, if we ever meet again
For the first time
On a blank sheet, with a new start.

7. "Ashamed"

I love you more than I hate my mistakes
And trust me, that's more than you could imagine
And I'm toothless because the facts hit the face like fists
And I am so ashamed of my shame,
Of how I feel so shunned into being quiet
A lesson learned can be translated into,
"You now have a hundred more things to learn
Without the chance to take a breath."

"Happily ever after" are words you and I write alike
When the sun goes down on hopefulness
And when restlessness rears its crooked grin
When the credits roll
And the words on the back of a hardcover child's book kiss you with the end
When the story becomes too much to handle, the monsters so real
You could swear you felt them sink their teeth into your deepest insecurities
But I am a man who loves using the words
"You, them, they, that man and those people"
Rather than, "me, myself, I"
Even though I've become obsessed with saying them all
Because I've come to the conclusion that
Overcoming and finding acceptance
For the actions and decisions of those gray matters that forgot what it was like
to feel
Is so much easier than accepting and admitting to yourself
How you haven't accomplished a fifth of what you dreamed
When four fifths of the time you're too busy listening
To the whispers of those you've accepted,
The ones who will never accept you.
So once again I say the word

"AND"

I want to break my heart open with this typewriter
Puncture it with this writing device
So maybe what will spill out can tell me how to express
All the things I'm fighting against
Maybe I can pick up the broken and cracked but beating muscle

And drink the understanding I used to know
Maybe if I break my heart open,
I can find the even younger boy who once felt bad
For every homeless, beaten, crying, lost, fallen, forgotten, missing, lost and
romantic soul
That ever had to fall in line with a world that tells you
Not to feel whatever isn't being felt by the person next to you
I wish I had a dictionary to look up every single word
To express to you how much hurt this world can give
When somebody wants to be hopeful
I wish my vocabulary ran quicker than my mouth
To try and find some phrase
Which would crack you open into realizing how poorly we treat each other
Because I'm far too uptight when you only hold me upright
For another belittling rant of how nonsensical it is to put words on paper
To recapture a moment
To make somebody have a feeling
To find a connection with somebody you've never met for a living
So now I get to write from a place I'd rather not
One where phone lines aren't used to tell these gray matters
"All is well because you're well off alive"
To give them color, bring them life
When the inventions of the modern man is used to tell a man
He's not enough of a man
And criticism, cynicism, and clearly a lot more "ISMS" are used
To tear you down into ripping phone cords out of walls we build up
Only so those near us don't tear us down.
For there is such a reason I have come to this conclusion
I'm really not toothless
My teeth have just been colored over charcoal black with this pencil
From the too many times that I chewed the lead in my mouth
Simply because you will never have me write down,
"Happily ever after, The End"
For there is no such thing
Just a day survived, a lesson learned
And a heart mended
No matter how many times you've tried to beat it open.

8. "Inches of a Canvas"

Where was I
When 'hateful wreck"
Turned into "insecure mess?"
I think it was when I came to the realization
That there's just no difference between them
I've been laying at this same intersection for years
Maybe one day I'll build a life around it
Chances are, writing like addiction will leave you broke, hungry, and alone
I don't know where I'm going with this
Just excuse me while I go dumpster diving for words
Searching for meaning amongst the filth
I have to find something
Because there's nothing
When you sit up and wonder if you and yours
Will ever make anything of yourselves
When an idea that not even you seem to get
Because others seem to just think you're strumming
And giving a speech
So here's to another idea
Another try
And another story
From a broken hall
To empty VFW halls
Both keep the poison on tap
And the sad stories singing in a jukebox
That doesn't need a quarter to play
Just any set of eyes you can find who look like they might listen
And you know what?
I see that I, myself, am responsible for so many of my problems
But then there is you
I see the women you'll become
So young, but I read middle-aged all over your face
I connect the cracks in what should have been smile lines
If my fingerprints found security around your face
It would break upon contact
You're not shallow, you just don't care
And I'm finding out the difference
I loved looking at your eyes and seeing so little

I hated myself for it
Especially when writing about you, and all I can say is, "I"
I shouldn't be bitter
Or fall head over heels for your misfortune
You look like a gypsy that's been on the road too long
Inhaling every ounce of dust on dirt roads walked
You lost soul
You gypsy
You harlot
You ice queen
Your wandering has worn you down
It's all over your face
The ugly on the inside
Has finally crawled out
Sell me something beautiful
Something you're not
And that's the beauty of the artist
Their work isn't found in a moment of time
A picture or a song
It's about finding a big enough canvas
To write out your love and disgust
I fear I'll never find one big enough
No color ugly enough
No sheet deep enough
As I slam the brush from the fist in the page
The ink always runs through eventually
But I keep going
I have to
Better to be painful than empty
It's the empty sheet that disgusts me
We're only here for a moment in time
Use every chance you can to teach something new
The beautiful and the ugly are the same thing
When you're writing out your story
I'll write until it's gone
Even then
I'll start ripping myself apart
To paint the pictures I feel
Until I'm nothing
In my last moments, I'll rip my heart out

For one last finger painting
Put that up on your refrigerator
Signed with a handprint
Sealed with the end
So if I cut my losses now
I'd be cutting off this life support
The line goes flat
And that obnoxious noise is the last thing I hear
I spent a life trying to tune it all out
And now the finale is the loudest of all
I fear moments like this
When I wish
I am lower than hope
Lower than faith
Beyond hell
And I cut to the core of nothing
The knuckles of miracle never tapped on my door
They never beat my door like we beat ourselves
Until the blood streaked across the wood
Screaming for me
Rap, tap, tap
Nothing
And so I think they're only stories
That I have over-romanticized
Broken women become goddesses
In the land of make-believe
The land I wish I,
I wish I,
I wish I
Never made up
Why do I ask myself for things I can't give to myself?
When I ask questions I know have no answers
My own voice bounces off these walls
It's the only knock on my door
Visitors are few and far these day
You were never on

9. "Ghost"

The next time you see me
I pray I'm bleeding from the head
And I've been confessing to this brick wall for hours
Once upon a time
This never existed
So now you feed
With a never-ending appetite
Or at least I hope
When I'm shoving what little remains
Down the throat of nothing
The never you knew was coming
What I should have seen miles away
I feel it from the pit of my stomach
It crawls up through me
Grabbing onto anything it can
Pushing upward
Until it's lodged in my brain
Making its home between the heart and the mind
Whispering to me
That this is the part where I give in
To worship at this makeshift altar
Where anger is praised
And I can't seem to find where I begin and my childhood ends
I see you in me in the worst of ways
Or maybe you just didn't have any good qualities to give
Even then, it's just an excuse to give in to cursed tongues
They hold the ability to make people disappear
I alienate everyone
It's the thing in me that wants to destroy myself
It's starting from the inside out
It wants no audience
It wants me to be alone
So nobody will stop it when it comes crawling out
Ripping me apart
I need to stop
Even if the known is what I fear
When we all just rip ourselves apart
But give innocent bystanders villainous roles

When I can't accept that it's just like you
Even though I could have sworn that I was nothing like you
Denial wastes time
But if I'm going to look inward for answers
Find the new story
The real beginning of me
But I don't think it starts with
Hoping and praying
They're just words
A product of the manmade machine
The mind
Yet we put everything into it
To take ourselves out of it
There's a need
To take a step back
And see things for what they really are
Places are just places
Yet we give them individual memories
Selfish creatures
Make home in the head where the feet meet stone
And that's why we'll never forget every taste of sadness
Every bit of pain
A lesson I haven't learned
One I haven't even bothered studying
Until I grow up
Come one step closer to the realization
That home is where the heart is
The inward
The one
The now
Go
But I don't know where anything is anymore

10. "Addiction"

Why doesn't this feel right?
I've been burning this bridge for years
And I live off the heat I get
From smelling the burning scent of everybody I knew
In a day that made a lot of sense
Brick by brick
Stone thrown by flesh hit
I'm stuck in a time where everything collapses forever
But nothing crashes
Waiting for the sound or scent of the end
Never arrives
Just constantly trying to get there
The smell too far to truly seduce
But close enough to make you want to bash your own face in
So you won't have to sit with the godforsaken time
That laughs at your fingertips when you're inches from its grace
So when am I saved
I just want you to see me for everything I could be
When I couldn't let go of everything you weren't
I could have sworn I was grasping at the dirt you now lived under
But I'm just burying myself in snow
Torture isn't an eternity of pain
Or some bloodbath seen of ripped-off limbs of vessels burst from the body
It's falling into the cracks of hope
And not being able to climb up
Bursting into flames in a dried up lake
And the people you've pushed away
Are a second too far to hear you scream for relief
It's the moment you come to the conclusion that you can't do it alone
Nobody is around to see the look in your eyes of "Finally, I get it."
Bruised.
Broken.
Bleeding.
Breathless.
With no one around to let you find rest
There is just you
There just is
You came from nature

And it doesn't really care when you come back, where or what for
Not a moment in time passes with the soil wanting to help you stay with it
Come back when you may
Let your body be blown in whatever direction the wind chooses this day
And nor does it care
What was the last living thought you had
I grabbed for you every goddamn day
I reached for something
Coming up with nothing
Because I walked too far away
Pushed too hard
Didn't try hard enough
And that's all I come up with
When I'm searching for all of you
Digging in the back of my memories for an image
That doesn't reflect the moment
But all I come up with is a lot of personal fault
And I'd love to put a happier thought in the head of death
But I always come back to this avenue
Each stone thrown down this block
Fills me with
A lot of personal regret
And poor decision making
When I was reaching for you
I found the real sad truth about me
So this is where I live
A million moments replay in a millisecond
When I feel the soil I become
When I come apart of what doesn't care

11. "Purgatory"

And at the end of the day
When most find an end to temporary doubts
I am only given a blessed cursed of hardened hands
That easier pick through that which brings me unrest

Even if I find this at the risk of no longer feeling what I once held dearly
Allow me to be a martyr brought upon a curse of my own thought
With an audience of only me, myself, and I
Truly, for such self-doubt, I may as well throw these rocks into the mirror
For reflections no longer bear a nature in which I feel I truly posses
Then again, weighed down by my own mind, heavy hands brought on by
another sunrise I must witness from a window I wish I could erase
I no longer even know if this is something I truly have in my possession
Or if my actions of past have gripped my future and don't allow me to better
today
I wish I could pick out my eyes and glass over all I have seen in twenty-one plus
Frame them for all to see
Put them on display to a world I don't think will quite understand.
Place every misspent moment in my sockets and enclose my skin over them
"Son, you are not blind, you are just too afraid to open your eyes."

It seems I can't wait to lose
What I've been searching for
As soon as I grab hold of it
Or so I tell myself when I think
That nobody attends the funeral of the nowhere and nothing martyr
So when I'm gone
Burn it, bury it, I don't care
You won't see me leave
As I laugh myself to the grave
Or the urn
Or the sea
The dumpster
Or wherever you feel is best
When it's over
After I search for all the ghosts that haunted me in my life
So I may finally meet them

Why could I have not saved my sight?
Why did I plague my visions with repetition of where I am?
But due to the fear of where I could have gone, here I rest
Fear is the nails that dig through my hands
Complacency is the blood that drips onto fingers
That have far too long ran themselves over pictures and portraits,
Of days I held myself in higher power
Awakened in pain from the aching stomach
That doesn't wish to feel the cold air of another day
I wish I could see the audience that I never had
I hope for the opposite-ended hammer
To erase me from this prison of self and these nails of doubt
First time, I try and open my eyes.

I fear not the ripping of metal off my skin
But rather the unknown fall I will take right after
Do I really wish to stay burdened with pain, to merely avoid the unknown?
Is it even remotely possible for what awaits me in shadows
To be worse than what tears at me in the daylight?
I have the rest of this life to allow my mind to run over the sight I lost
Because your sun, I could not stop staring at.
And this..
This answer is no longer enough to comfort me
In my freeform bitterness
Please, allow my back a better burden in this short lifetime
Rather than an eternity of weighing down my own empty eyes
How many more days will I live as a ghost with hardened hands
Rather than a man that feels all the pains of his hard work?

Until I realize
I'll never come across
What I only made up in my head
Isn't it funny that our fears are only a projection
Of what we make up in our own heads?
Yeah, I'm laughing
Wherever I am

12. "Dead Ends"

I once saw an angel fly away
She landed on a cloud of pollution
But called it heaven
Reached the tainted utopia on heroin-filled syringes
She whispered in my ear before she left
I smelled the truth on her mouth
Felt the words on her tongue
"You're ruinous to your own well-being."
After that, I set myself free and let go of the lie
I'll let you know when I get to the bottom, ghost of mine.
To the bottom of what?

How about nothing?
Maybe I am just getting old
Or bitter
It just seems like the truth holds such little value anymore
A herd mentality still
Even though the blades in the slaughterhouse haven't slowed
The blood still wet
It has yet to coagulate around my throat
I walk in your home day after day
And still I'm greeted with the same old same old
There are no angels, and you're just a dead end
Hide behind forgiveness
When there's nowhere to
You can't see the bars
And the prison is one lifetime long
You can't measure that in miles
When the end of the road holds nothing dear
A storybook child
With an oven end

We write our love but the world is just illiterate in the end
I don't believe in angels
But I believe the holes in your arms
There's no horned pitchfork ready to impale
Yet there are dead hollow eyes that pissed themselves and died
So much uglier in the end and in truth

But since when did that stop us?
They can call you a goddess in the flesh
Forgiveness awaiting birth
Yet you aborted it yourself and cried wolf
Oh, what big teeth you have
Oh, what grand lies they tell
Clenched in between my heart and my eyes
Save the dramatics
Grind them to the bone
And I'll just sharpen my teeth
Behind this door
Beneath my tongue
Until I realize
There was no angel
There was no you
And I haven't seen a single soul since I got here
Confessing to myself
All the blame I scream disgusts me
From Nothing, Comes Nothing
A world alone, I made for myself
Living on Dead Ends
What beauty
What repetition
When is there rebirth?
In a land of one
Alone

Here I am again

www.ingramcontent.com/pod-product-compliance
Lightning Source LLC
Chambersburg PA
CBHW051830090426
42736CB00011B/1736